IT'S THE END OF THE WORLD

But What Are We Really Afraid Of?

Adam Roberts

Elliott&Thompson

First published 2020 by
Elliott and Thompson Limited
2 John Street
London WC1N 2ES
www.eandtbooks.com

ISBN: 978-1-78396-474-1

9 8 7 6 5 4 3 2 1

A catalogue record for this book is available from the British Library.

Typesetting by Marie Doherty
Printed in the UK by TJ Books Ltd

CONTENTS

Introduction: The End is Nigh   I

1. Escaping the Wrath of the Gods: 23
    Religious Doomsday

2. A Swarm of Undead: The Zombie   55
    Apocalypse

3. Bring Out Your Dead: World-ending   79
    Plagues

4. The Age of the Machine: Technology   107
    Unleashed

5. Heat Deaths and Eternal Returns: 131
    The End of the Universe

6. The World on Fire: Climate Armageddon   155

    Epilogue: The End is Never   181

    Index   195

INTRODUCTION

THE END IS NIGH

It's always the end of the world. Human cultures around the globe have been obsessed with this ultimate ending for thousands of years. Religious sects insist, as they have always done, that God is moments away from rolling up the scroll of the universe and exterminating us all. And secularists are no more optimistic: according to popular culture, an alien invasion is always poised to wipe out human civilisation, or our own technology has risen up to obliterate us in the form of armies of chromium robots or sinister computer programs. An asteroid with our name on it is hurtling towards us even as we speak. Scientists warn of impending climate catastrophe, and books and films flesh out those warnings with floods, famines and new global ice ages. Plagues and new diseases are queuing up to infect us all. I started writing this book before Covid-19 shut down societies across the globe, but I'm finishing it from inside that lockdown. The pandemic has been an alarming and surreal experience for all of us, but I feel it has been slightly more on-the-nose for me, having watched my speculation about world-ending plagues and collective disasters coming true all around me.*

This book asks why we are so fascinated by the end of the world and starts from the fact that I myself have long been intrigued by it. As you might imagine, I've thought quite a lot about why that might be. Writing this book has crystallised these thoughts; I now wonder if my personal engagement with apocalypse might have something to do with my profession. I write science fiction. A writer necessarily takes a professional interest in the structure of storytelling, which is to

---

* I hope, therefore, my next book will be about why we should give balding, middle-aged writers in Berkshire millions of pounds and our collective adulation.

say: in beginnings, middles and ends. Knowing how a story ends tells us much about the way the story began and unfolded; it helps us to see what was important. Apocalypse is not only the ultimate end but is also always bound up with beginnings and middles, in much the same – if somewhat more complex – way. And while some writers concentrate on individuals and the personal aspect of living and dying, science fiction writers tend to project out from the individual to inter-planetary, even the galactic and universal.

Perhaps this starts to explain why stories about the end of the world are so ubiquitous in popular culture. From the Apocalypse of St John to *Dr. Strangelove*, from H. G. Wells's *Time Machine* to *The Omega Man*, from plagues of zombies and space viruses to the giant blue planet of Lars von Trier's *Melancholia* crashing into Earth, what does it say about us? Why did the press go into hysterics in 2012 at the idea that the Mayan cal-endar, carved in Mesoamerican stone over 5,000 years ago, came to an end on 21 December of that year? Though this low-rent apocalyptic frenzy now looks fool-ish, at the time it generated much excitement as the date approached. Why?

It is not, I think, because we are morbid, pessimistic or masochistic; on one level it's perfectly sensible to be interested in the end of the world. There are lots of beginnings in life, but to quote from the Matrix movie trilogy, 'Everything that has a beginning has an end.' We are all mortal, and we will all die. One way of understanding our fascination with the end of the world is that such stories project our personal mortality onto the world. Just as we will each die, so the whole world will die at some point.

There's a Latin phrase for it: *timor mortis*, the fear of dying. We think about the end of the world – we speculate about it, write books and make films about it – as a way of thinking about the end of our individual lives. Unique among animals, it seems, we are aware of our mortality. As you read this sentence, you are drawing air into your lungs but you also know that one day you will draw your final breath. It's an alarming thing, but there's no avoiding it. In the words of seventeenth-century poet and preacher John Donne, 'Death comes equally to us all, and makes us all equal when it comes.' The twentieth-century writer and critic G. K. Chesterton expanded upon this point:

> There are two things in which all men are manifestly and unmistakably equal. They are not equally clever or equally muscular or equally fat, as the

sages of the modern reaction (with piercing insight) perceive. But this is a spiritual certainty, that all men are tragic . . . No special and private sorrow can be so dreadful as the fact of having to die.*

Chesterton is discussing Walter Scott here – not a novelist whose reputation has particularly survived into the twentieth century, although a name you have surely heard; millions of passengers pass through Edinburgh Waverley Station every year, overlooked by the Scott monument and named after his first novel.† What Chesterton loved about him was his grasp of 'the graver basis' of our common humanity, 'the dark dignity of man':

'Can you find no way?' asks Sir Arthur Wardour of the beggar when they are cut off by the tide. 'I'll give you a farm . . . I'll make you rich.' . . . 'Our riches will soon be equal,' says the beggar, and looks out across the advancing sea.

---

*   G. K. Chesterton, *Dickens* (1906), Chapter 10.

†   Similarly, the Edinburgh football club Heart of Midlothian FC (or simply 'Hearts') is named after one of Scott's best novels, *The Heart of Midlothian* (1818).

Chesterton is right to pick out that moment from Scott's *The Antiquary*, which sends a shiver up my spine. Maybe we've turned our lives to riches, or perhaps we've lived as beggars, whether materially or spiritually. The latter is perhaps more likely, and the more we feel we have wasted our life, the stronger we want to cling on to it. And the step from individual mortality to collective mortality becomes a simple extrapolation. If a person can die, so can a people. If a life can end, so can a world. And so we speculate.

There are two broad approaches in imagining the apocalypse. The first kind of story shows us the ending as a final terminus, Elvis finally leaving the building, and this time forever. In this category, we find accounts by astrophysicists of the ultimate fate of the universe, but also grim fantasies by writers like Byron and H. G. Wells that are bleakly unremitting.

The second kind of story is, surprisingly, much more common. These are works that represent the end of the world but make an exception for a chosen few; stories in which a handful of people survive the end of all things in a redoubt, or who slip away from the catastrophe through some magic escape hatch and start again. In Neal Stephenson's novel *Seveneves* (2015), for example, something – we're not told what, but it might be a passing black hole – rips the moon to fragments, making the annihilation of life on Earth inevitable thanks to a 'Hard Rain' of fragments that continues for 5,000 years. It looks like a pretty comprehensive ending of the world. However, Stephenson imagines a point beyond the end of all things in order to tell his story. He describes various small groups of people fleeing Earth in spaceships or lurking at the bottom of the ocean in submarines and then, with a bravura jump-cut, takes us fifty centuries into the future, when the survivors start recolonising the ruined Earth. In this type of story, it's the end of the world as we know it but, somehow, we feel fine.

These two approaches reflect two main human responses to our mortality. Some of us accept our fate, either gloomily or stoically, believing it to be our final end; but others believe that the end won't actually be the end – that we will somehow survive the ending.

Consider, for example, the recent boom in apocalypse insurance. You can take out insurance for pretty much anything, but lately some people have been insuring themselves against the end of the world.* It seems

---

* 'According to Angelo Robles, founder and CEO of the Family Office Association, "taking steps to deal with the apocalypse is

like a win–win for the insurance companies – if the world doesn't end they don't have to pay out, and if it does there will be nobody left to make a claim. The customers taking out the insurance must be crazy, right? Not necessarily. Insurance, after all, is buying peace of mind. Behind the policy specifics of financial reimbursement is the more fundamental consideration that there will be an afterwards in which insurance claims can be negotiated. Insurance is a mode of hope, which is our best protection in the face of extinction. Who knows? Maybe the end of the world will be a partial rather than a total phenomenon. Maybe the smart ones are those who gamble that the end of the world might be the beginning of something else.

This attitude to apocalypse, it turns out, is so far from uncommon as to be the default. St John's Revelation at the end of the Bible rains a series of terrible destructions upon the world, obliterating life many times over, only to cap his narrative with a surprise new

becoming a bigger concern among many family offices. We're seeing more members and executives talking about the possibility and trying to work out the likelihood of different scenarios so they can decide how intensely to address the matter."' Russ Alan Prince, 'Many of the Super-Rich and Family Offices are buying "Apocalypse Insurance"', *Forbes*, 26 September 2017.

earth and a new heaven, a paradise for the chosen few. The same is true of the Norse myth of Ragnarök, of the film *Children of Men* and of George A. Romero's zombie movie *Dawn of the Dead*. It's true also of the 1998 video game *Apocalypse* and the alien invasion movie *Independence Day* (1996). It seems to me that there is an interesting paradox at work here: the end is final, and yet it also represents a strange new beginning.

This is partly down to a problem we encounter when we try to imagine the end – whether of the world or our own lives. We can only think from *inside* our own minds – everything we think and feel comes framed by our experiences and assumptions. No person can magically step outside their own personhood and think purely objective thoughts. We can obviously be a little more or less objective in how we think about things, but absolute objectivity is always compromised by the fact that the thinking is being undertaken by a subject.

Death is an important case of this. We can imagine dying, but we cannot imagine *being dead* because that, by definition, means the absence of the thinking subject. Death is not something that is lived through. Subjectivity is baked in to how we think, in the sense that we can't remove it and keep thinking. We can, of course, imagine some of the things of life being taken away by death: light being replaced by darkness, movement being replaced by motionlessness, and so on. But we can't imagine *imagining* being taken away. We can't think about the absence of thought, by definition.

As a result, we tend to think of being dead as just another kind of being alive. We may think dying brings us out of life and to rainbow-threaded cloudy cities, with the twanging of harps. Or we may think of death as being like life, but less so: cold, denuded and bare – lying inside a coffin forever, unable to move. The Greeks thought of the afterlife in such terms. For Homer, the souls of the dead continue to exist, but in a grim, shadowy place, drained of both *menos* (strength) and *phrenes* (wit). Something similar is true in the Hebrew Bible, where both the righteous and the unrighteous dead go to the same dark place, 'Sheol': a lightless place cut off from life and separated from God.

But both the cliché of Christian heaven and this gloomier pre-Christian afterlife illustrate the same problem: the inability of thought to let go of the fact that it is thinking and the fallacy that we will somehow still be around after we have stopped being around. If stopping being is *still being*, then being hasn't stopped.

I don't say this to mock you for your beliefs if you happen to believe that death is a gateway to some new kind of life, to a heaven or reincarnation – you could well be right to believe such things.* My point, rather, is how we *represent* this end – both individual death, and the death of the world – in art and culture. And so far as that is concerned, the tenacity of our imagination becomes the defining feature of the end of the world. That is why so many imagined versions of the end of the world portray a cosmos that stubbornly persists as it ends, and even after it has ended. It is almost always the case that apocalypse leads us into a transcendent realm, in which the miseries of life have passed away.

And so we turn our end into a beginning.

* * *

* I think it becomes clear in what follows that I do not believe my individual consciousness will survive my death. Indeed, the real worry for me is not that I won't survive death, but precisely that *I might* – because the prospect of living forever fills me with a far greater sense of existential dread than the prospect of stopping. I daresay it is bad theology, but I'm rather drawn to the idea that God became Christ in order to put an end to his own endlessness. 'God is growing bitter,' Jacques Rigaut said in 1920. 'He envies man his mortality.'

When we're talking about the end of the world, are we talking about the front end or the back end? Lots of things have both, from trains and snakes to conga lines. But thinking about 'the end of the world' in this context imparts a strange spin to the notion. I'm going to assume that your first thought was that it is the world's back end. It is, after all, the last bit that we will encounter before it's all over, the curtain call, the fag end, the last page of the book. But what if the end of the world is actually the *front* end? After all, it's something that happens in time, and it's hardly an original observation to note that we do not travel forward in time. You might think we do, but consider this: if we *were* travelling forward in time, we'd be able to see where we're going. The fact that we can only see where we've already been means we must be moving backwards through time, hurtling in reverse one second per second with our backs to our destination.

If the idea of apocalypse as the *front* end of the world seems counter-intuitive, maybe you've been thinking in the wrong direction.* You've been assuming that we start in some place 'in time' – like John Bunyan's City

---

* Thinking in the wrong direction is like looking in the wrong direction, but for thinking.

of Destruction, the beginning of Dorothy's yellow brick road or the first square of the board game The Game of Life – and then walk forward from there, along our path, through various adventures, until we reach our destination: our Emerald City. But what if, instead of moving forwards, we are moving backwards? We can reach our arms back a little way and grope into our immediate future, but we can't turn our heads far enough around to see where we are going. Despite this, we have no option but to keep going, our backs to our destination. We can see our past – indeed, most of us are hypnotised by the view and stare at it, whether longingly (it looks so much nicer than where we presently are) or in horror (such trauma!). For many of us, what we can see absorbs our attention, but where we are going is not visible. That fact ought to occupy our minds a little more than it does – we are moving backwards into our lives, with no real sense of what is behind us. Maybe it's a clear, uncluttered road, or maybe we are about to crash into a brick wall.

Asking why we are engaged in this crazy behaviour is tantamount to asking why we exist. We run because the alternative is to be motionless, which is not being alive at all. So whether we run with the vigour of youth or the exhaustion of age, we run, and this is just how things are. We are all running together, and in a direction we can't see. From time to time, individuals stumble and fall and their race is over, but the rest of us continue our bizarre backwards marathon.

What is behind us? Where will the race come to an end? And how far behind us is it? Maybe the pothole of a heart attack will trip us up, or perhaps a stretch of quicksand named 'cancer' will bog us down. Maybe we'll keep running until our legs give out and we fall, or maybe we will tumble over a cliff edge into an abyss. Maybe the absolute end to the race for everyone is right behind us. We can never know. All we can know is that it's there and try to make our peace with it.

* * *

We all deal with our knowledge of mortality in different ways. We might simply ignore it, although that's not a very healthy way of living. The brute fact of it might make us fearful, or we might find a kind of existential tranquillity in its inevitability.

My personal preference for handling it – humour – is not universally popular, and you may decide that my larger arguments about the end of the world here are undermined by my predilection for joking. To each their own.

I can hardly defend my own 'jokes', several examples of which you have already encountered if you've read this far, but I would note that humour looms large in the story of the apocalypse. This is why so much apocalyptic fantasy is so kitsch and over-the-top, so melodramatic and heightened. A book like Terry Pratchett and Neil Gaiman's *Good Omens* (1990) styles the apocalypse of St John as comedy, combining satire and a broader comic sensibility into something that is both profound and hilarious. Seth Rogen and Evan Goldberg's *This Is the End* (2013) treats the same topic with vulgar slapstick and cynicism. Kubrick's *Dr. Strangelove* (1964) treats the end of the world by nuclear war as black comedy. 'You've got to laugh,' as the adage has it, 'or you'd cry.'

My approach in this book is comic, but that does not mean it is not serious – I'm not trying to make light of what is often a painful matter, and I have attended too many funerals to be dismissive of bereavement. But comedy, because it reshapes contradiction and paradox into hilarity and makes our fears pleasurable, seems to me precisely the right way to address the issue of apocalypse.

Fantasies of the end take many different approaches: funny, inventive, ghastly, far-fetched and scarily realistic. It is fertile territory for our imaginations. But if we look more closely at the way we tell our stories, we can see that *how* we portray the end can also tell us much about how we understand the world and the people around us, not just about how we think about our mortality. They can illustrate our dread of judgement, the importance we place on our societal connections, the darker side of our own human nature. From religious doomsdays and swarms of monsters to biological plague and technological doom, from the winding down of the universe to environmental catastrophe, in these pages we'll explore not just our fear of death, but more importantly all the things we're really afraid of in life.

But first I need to persuade you that the title of this introduction is correct: the world is going to end much sooner than you think. But first, like a stock character from a cartoon walking the streets wearing a sandwich board bearing the legend THE END IS NIGH, I need to persuade you that the title of this introduction is correct: the world is going to end much sooner than you think. Humans have predicted the end of the world for thousands of years, yet it is always presented as imminent. If it appears contradictory to suggest that something can be imminent for millennia that's because it is – imminent means that it's happening very soon, and there's nothing immediate about a timespan of tens of centuries. In the words of the Smiths, how soon *is* now?

So the question is this: is the end of the world millions of years away, or will it arrive momentarily?

According to the discipline of statistical probability, there is a scientific way of weighing up whether the world will end tomorrow or in trillions of years in the future, and the news is not good. I'm talking about the so-called 'Doomsday argument', which uses Bayesian probability to assess the odds of whether the world will end sooner or later.*

Probability, of course, is to do not with certainty but likelihood. Roll a die once and you have a one-in-six chance of guessing the number correctly; but roll a die a million times and the *probability* that each number will appear with one-sixth of throws increases. If you rolled the die a billion times and plotted how often each number appeared on a bar chart, you would have a chart in which all six bars were the same height. Probability is what happens when random instances accumulate

---

* A good recent explanation of this position is John Leslie's *The End of the World: The Science and Ethics of Human Extinction* (Routledge, 1996). I have taken the 'lottery ball' analogy from Leslie.

to the point where randomness cancels itself out and the underlying pattern is revealed.

Bayes' theorem is a branch of probability theory named after its inventor, the eighteenth-century English clergyman Thomas Bayes. Here's how it works. If I asked you the likelihood that it was raining outside, you could go to the window and look; then you could tell me directly. However, let's say that you're too far from the window to see whether it's raining, but you can see that lots of people outside have opened their umbrellas. Though this doesn't absolutely confirm that it is raining, the alternatives are less likely than the most probable explanation.

That's a trivial example, but there are plenty of non-trivial ways in which Bayesian reasoning is applied in the real world. For example, our likelihood of getting certain cancers increases under the influence of factors such as age, gender and lifestyle. Knowing this, doctors can use Bayes' theorem to assess the probability of such cancers and so improve prevention and increase survival rates. In other words, feeding certain kinds of observation into Bayes' theorem, in a medical context, can literally save lives.

What does this have to do with the end of the world? Well, a group of statistically minded philosophers recently used Bayes' theorem to calculate the probability that the world is about to end. This was an exercise in probability theory rather than a specific prophecy. The idea was not to point the finger directly at environmental collapse, nuclear war or alien invasion but to establish the larger likelihoods of extinction. They did not feed data concerning the amount of carbon dioxide in the atmosphere or the number of nuclear weapons in the world into Bayes' theorem; they fed into it only the fact *that we are alive now*. When they did that, the equation generated an intriguing result: the probability that human beings will become extinct in the relatively near future increased.

It is, of course, rational to be concerned that environmental stability is collapsing, or that nuclear weapons could, whether by accident or design, wreak terrible harm upon our world. But this hypothesis increases the likelihood of human extinction *irrespective of other data*. To be clear: the end of the world to which this analysis relates (because, of course, there are several different kinds of end of the world) is one in which there are no more humans alive, not in which the planet itself is necessarily destroyed. As humans, this really ought to concern us. Sensible people are right to have specific concerns – for instance, that the thawing of frozen methane in Siberia and the release of that greenhouse gas into the atmosphere makes the imminent end of a human-habitable world more likely. OK. The point of this analysis is: if we factor in Bayes' theory, we should revise our estimate of that probability, whatever it is, *upwards*. It's a strange, even a counter-intuitive, argument, but that doesn't necessarily mean it's wrong.

Consider two hypotheses: 'Doom Soon', the belief that human history will end in the near future and 'Doom Delayed', the belief that *Homo sapiens* will survive long into the future. In the latter scenario, the population of all humans who will ever live will be very large, maybe trillions of people in total. In the case of 'Doom Soon', that number will be much lower, because the ending of the world will prevent more humans being born. Using Bayes' theorem, statisticians estimate the respective probabilities of the two scenarios and conclude that the probability that you are living right now is greater if 'Doom Soon' is true and less probable if 'Doom Delayed' is true.

Think of it like this: you being born exactly when you were born is a matter of chance, like picking a lottery ball from a giant tub of such balls. If half the balls in our notional tub are black and half are white, there's a 50 per cent chance of picking either colour. Equal probabilities. That's simple enough.

But imagine that you have to pick a random ball from a tub that contains either ten or one hundred balls, with each ball numbered sequentially from one to one hundred. In goes your hand and out comes ball number three. Now, is it more likely that the tub contains ten or one hundred balls? Bayes' theorem tells us that you picking ball number three makes it more likely the tub contains ten balls, because the probability of picking ball number three is higher if the tub contains ten balls than if it contains one hundred – ten times higher, in fact. It doesn't *prove* that the tub contains ten balls, of course – maybe it contains a hundred and you just happened to pick ball number three – but it does make the ten-ball hypothesis more likely.

Now apply this thought experiment to the end of the world. Let's say that I am the 50 billionth human being born on Planet Earth. 'Doom Soon' might say that the number of humans who will ever live will be 100 billion, while 'Doom Delayed' says that number will be much larger – 1,000 billion, perhaps. But the fact that I've picked a ball with the number 50 billion written on it means that 'Doom Soon' is more likely than 'Doom Delayed', just as picking out ball number three in the example above makes it more likely that there are ten rather than one hundred balls in the tub.

There's another statistical principle to take into account here: the *we-are-not-special* doctrine. People used to believe that the Earth was at the centre of the universe and that the Sun and the stars revolved around us, until Copernicus changed that view. It turns out that we are not the centre around which the entire cosmos revolves, but are rather a planet orbiting a small star that itself is in the outer reaches of the spiral arm of one of many billions of galaxies. Across a wide range of sciences, the beliefs that used to mark *Homo sapiens* out as unique and special have shifted.

The end of the world has its own equivalent argument. Consider 'Doom Delayed': perhaps humanity will colonise the universe, live for billions of years and produce trillions of human beings. If that is true, you and I have popped up extremely early in the human story – what are the odds of that? We would expect, by probabilistic distribution, to be somewhere in the middle. That leads our analysis towards the idea of 'Doom Soon' – not that the world is going to end by this coming midnight (that would also be unlikely) but that it is going to end over the next couple of centuries. Probabilistically speaking, the end of the world *is* nigh.

ESCAPING THE WRATH OF THE GODS: RELIGIOUS DOOMSDAYS

O f all the types of stories that humanity has told itself about the end of the world, religious apocalypse is the oldest and most enduring. From the four horsemen of the Christian apocalypse, the seven suns of Buddhist eschatology and the chilly Ragnarök cosmocide in Norse mythology, the religions that posit a cosmos-creator also posit a cosmos-destroyer. For most of them, these two figures are one and the same.

As we've already discussed, imagining the end of the world is one of the ways in which we imagine our own mortality as individuals. One important function served by religion is to provide structure and consolation in the face of our individual mortality; and so it also offers a way we can make sense of the end of everything.

Let's start with the conventional understanding of this story. In the Jewish and Christian tradition, God made the universe in six days and rested on the seventh. Since then, our story has been unfolding in all its glorious complexity. However, a story without an ending is an unsatisfying prospect and if God can create the world, he might also be tempted to unmake it, to tear it down and destroy it, with the virtuous going to heaven and the wicked to perdition. Something similar is true of the Islamic tradition, according to which there will be signs of the coming end times, but finally the sun will rise from the west and there will be three catastrophic 'sinkings of the earth' in the east, the west and in Arabia. Then the dead will return to life and a fire will flare in Yemen that will gather all to 'Mahshar Al Qiy'amah', the gathering for judgement, after which the faithful will go to heaven.

So when will this happen? According to believers, soon:

A recent poll showed that 41 per cent of Americans overall and 58 per cent of white evangelical Christians believe that Jesus will either 'probably' or 'definitely' return by 2050. Within the Muslim world, a 2012 poll found a similar prevalence of beliefs, with 83 per cent of Muslims in Afghanistan, 72 per cent in Iraq, and 68 per cent in Turkey anticipating the return of the Mahdi (the end-times messiah) in their lifetime.*

The end, it seems, is indeed nigh.

Why do these predictions so often take place in the here and now? The critic Frank Kermode argued that we are uncomfortable with the idea that our lives occupy a short period in the vastly longer history of the world. Stories of the end exist, he says, to give us the chance to consider our own lives and mortality, to make sense of our place in time and our relationship to the beginning and the end. 'It seems to be a condition attaching to the exercise of thinking about the future,' Kermode says, 'that one should assume one's own time

---

* Phil Torres, 'How religious and non-religious people view the apocalypse', *The Bulletin*, 18 August 2017.

to stand in extraordinary relation to it.'* And so 'men in the middest', as Kermode styles them, are fond of making predictions as to specific near-at-hand dates as to when the world will end. We fear being left out of the crucial climax of the story. Better nigh than never.

Still, our religious myths are about much more than providing ways to grapple with our mortality. While religion is often used to predict that the end is nigh, many of our religious stories about apocalypse are based in the past, and since we are still around, these prior ends of the world have clearly proved unsuccessful. If you believe that a god is capable of making a universe, you will also believe that he is capable of unmaking it, but if that is the case, why would there be so many unsuccessful attempts? It doesn't reflect well on the powerfulness of our various gods.

Is it always the case that someone who makes something can unmake it? The modern myth of Frankenstein speaks to our sense that making can entail not only horrible but irrevocable unintended consequences. We build nuclear reactors without knowing how to decommission them, and we produce trillions of tons of

* Frank Kermode, *The Sense of an Ending* (Oxford University Press, 1967), p. 8.

plastic and don't know how to get rid of it. Our creations assume a malign life of their own and start wrecking the joint. It may be that, as our attempts to wrest our world from the catastrophic climate change have suggested, this baleful truth will be revealed as the core certainty – that we can create but cannot uncreate. If that's true for us, why should it be any different for a god?

Of course our gods are more powerful than we are – omnipotence, surely, includes the power to undo what they have done – and yet from Greek myth to the Bible, religious stories are rife with divine creators deciding to unmake their creations and finding themselves unable to follow through on their divine resolution.

Greek myths in particular are filled with previous failed attempts by the gods. Take for example the legend of Prometheus.* Zeus, the story goes, repented of having created humankind after seeing the wickedness to which we are prone and decided to let us die out in the cold and hostile world before creating a better kind of

---

*   Since *Frankenstein* stands at the head of a long tradition of science fiction about scientific hubris, of stories of science creating something over which it loses control, it is worth noting that Mary Shelley subtitled her novel 'The New Prometheus'. She had a different myth about Prometheus in mind when she did this, but let's not split hairs. Or, indeed, livers.

creature. But Prometheus, a Titan (an entity not quite as elevated as an Olympian god, although still a powerful immortal), took pity on us and smuggled fire from the sun down to earth in a fennel stalk. We humans were thus able to prosper, and Zeus's plan to see us all dead was thwarted. He was so angry with Prometheus that he chained him to a rock high in the Caucasus Mountains, where, according to some versions of the myth, he remains. Every day an eagle flies down, rips open his belly with his beak and devours his liver; every night the liver miraculously regrows, so the punishment can begin again the next day.*

That Zeus takes his anger out on Prometheus in this savage manner is certainly in character, but we might wonder why, if he wanted humanity extirpated, he didn't focus on the task in hand – flocks of eagles and a rain of thunderbolts would surely go some way towards actively finishing us off. Or what about a flood?

In some versions of the myth, a flood is exactly what Zeus sends next; having failed to destroy humanity once, he resolves to drown us all. But Prometheus's mortal son Deucalion, warned by his father, has the foresight to build a giant chest big enough to fit

---

* Prometheus suffered profuse Zeus abuse.

himself, his wife and his family. In this manner he survives the flood, floating about for nine days and nights until the waters recede. Whatever else this myth is saying, I think we can all agree that it shows a lamentable sloppiness on Zeus's behalf. The father of the gods can summon floods to drown the whole world, but can't aim a single thunderbolt at a wooden box bobbing along on the waves? Perhaps the problem is that Zeus lacks not the capacity to finish off Deucalion but the inclination; although he knows he really ought to purge humanity from the world, he just can't bring himself to do it.

The Deucalion story has an obvious parallel with the story of Noah, in which God has had enough of human wickedness. In the Torah and the Old Testament, God decides that Noah will survive because he is the world's only righteous man, giving him advance warning of the coming flood. That is offered as an explanation for why God doesn't tie off the unfinished business that Noah represents.

The common feature in these narratives is that the gods decide to destroy us because they have grown increasingly disgusted with our human sinfulness. The point, in other words, is *punishment*, and if there aren't any people around afterwards to learn the lesson, what is the point of the punishment? So this is not as much about mortality as it is morality. We carry within ourselves, to varying degrees, a sense of personal discontent linked to shame and guilt. Only the sociopath is free of those two qualities; for most normal people they loom pretty large. We are afraid that our nature is inherently sinful and that, accordingly, we deserve what we get. These stories are a judgement on how a society has lost its way; cautionary tales to scare us into being good. If a person punishes us, then perhaps there has been some kind of miscarriage of justice. But that can't be true if God punishes us because God *is* justice.

There are versions of this particular end-of-the-world story – God's wrath – all over the globe: the flood that moves across the world like the bar of an Etch A Sketch, resetting it to blankness. The world is styled as emerging from the waters, just as we are each born when our mother's waters break, so there is a symmetry in the idea that the world will end with a flood. That such narratives speak to a general collective experience makes more sense than the idea that it relates to any historical event. There have, of course, been floods in the world's history, including some on a prodigious scale. It has been hypothesised that the Black Sea was created around 5600 BCE when a rise in global sea levels caused the Mediterranean to burst over a land barrier, turning a previous freshwater lake into a much larger saltwater sea. The marine geologists William Ryan and Walter Pitman have speculated that memories of this gigantic flood fed into the many flood narratives in Mesopotamia and the Near East, including the Biblical flood of Noah.* But there are reasons for avoiding such parochialism: flood narratives occur in mythologies from all around the world, and not just from the area around the Black Sea. Ours is a watery world, and most early human societies lived by or near seas and oceans. Floods happen in the real world; tides and tidal bores and tsunamis affect all coastlines. In a world before globalisation, with communities living in isolation, local events such as these would have seemed practically world-ending at the time. With no explanation other than an angry god, the stories and myths that emerged from these incidents are often replete with ideas of punishment and a world reborn into innocence.

Hindu mythology includes the story of a great flood called Pralaya. In this myth, the first man, Manu, gets

* William Ryan and Walter Pitman, *Noah's Flood: The New Scientific Discoveries about the Event that Changed History* (Simon & Schuster, 1999).

advanced warning of it from Vishnu and is able to construct a boat in which to escape. In Mesoamerica, the Tlapanec and Huastec peoples told stories of gods who drowned everybody, outraged at human iniquity. One man survives with his dog and, fortunately for the continuing existence of humankind, the dog possesses the ability to metamorphose into a woman at night, which allows them to repopulate the earth. In India, Puluga, the creator god of the Andaman peoples, punishes human wickedness with a devastating flood, but two men and two women survive in a boat. One of the earliest stories that survives from human prehistory, recorded in the *Epic of Gilgamesh* (written in 2100 BCE in Mesopotamia) concerns a great flood sent by the gods to wash the wickedness of humanity off the face of the world. This plan misfires because one of the gods, Ea, breaks ranks with the others and warns a human he favours: Utnapishtim. Ea tells him to build a boat so that his family and 'all the animals of the field' can be saved from the coming flood, and so he lives, ensuring the survival of humankind.

Many religions put a positive spin on these stories to gain adherents; God is punishing only those heretics and unbelievers, not us. For us there will be a little escape hatch through which we can make our way to a new heaven and a new earth. Our salvation tends to come in the form of a saviour figure, sent to guide the faithful through the end. The Jews are still waiting for their promised messiah, while Christians – who budded off from that ancient faith 2,000 years ago – believe the saviour came once and will return again. In fifth-century CE China, an unknown Taoist master wrote the *Divine Incantations Scripture*, which promises the coming of a messianic figure who will rule over the faithful and destroy the rest of humanity. The text talks about the end of the world as a battle between the gods, or the 'officials of the celestial bureaucracy', and 'daemon kings', a metaphysical war between order and chaos that will lead to the renewal of our terrestrial world.* We humans are exhorted to follow the tao, or 'way' – to live a moral life under the proper authorities with 'dynamic obedience'. This *Scripture* offers the assistance of heavenly 'ghost soldiers' to those who upheld its teachings. It was so popular that two centuries later many people

---

* 'According to the Chinese view, the circumpolar stars represent the palace surrounding the emperor, who is the pole star, and the various members of the celestial bureaucracy. Indeed, the Chinese saw the night sky as a mirror of the empire, and saw the empire as a mirror of the sky, on earth.' Alexus McLeod, *Astronomy in the Ancient World: Early and Modern Views on Celestial Events* (Springer, 2016), pp. 89–90.

believed the Han prince Li Hong was the promised messiah. His mother, alarmed that he would use his popular support to seize power, had him poisoned.

Not every story allows a loophole for the righteous. Norse myths of the end of the world tell a story that includes both gods and men in the coming disaster, something which neither can escape. It's also a flood, of sorts – an apocalypse of ice. According to this legendarium, Odin, the leader of the Norse gods, knows that one day soon the universe will come to an end. By way of preparing for this grim fate, he assembles an army of the bravest warriors – those who die valiantly in battle are collected by Odin's Valkyries and entertained at a feast in the halls of Valhalla. Odin wants these warriors on hand and ready to fight when the end times come: when giants, monsters and the huge sky wolf Fenrir will attack. At that time, Odin and his warriors will fight. They will not win, but that is not the point. Odin is well aware that they will lose, that Thor will be killed by the poisonous Midgard Serpent, that Odin's wife Frey will be killed by the fire monster Surt, and that Odin himself will be devoured by Fenrir. The sun will turn black, the stars will disappear, the earth will sink into the sea, steam will rise and flames will burn the heavens. People will flee in terror, though they are doomed wherever they go. What matters is not that we will lose, but *how* we lose – and that we go down fighting. It degrades one's dignity, according to Norse culture, to whine about suffering or reverses. They are inevitable. What matters is not *that* they happen, but how much defiance we can face them with, both in life and in death.

It is strangely fitting that this account of the inevitable death of the universe was almost lost to us. These stories, once passed about as the oral culture of early Scandinavians, had entirely died out by the Renaissance – there is no mention of them in any of Shakespeare's plays, for instance. But then in 1662, a bishop called Brynjólfur Sveinsson happened to come across a manuscript, written in Old Norse, in an Icelandic farmhouse. If this bundle of papers had been burnt, eaten by mice or otherwise discarded, we would have almost no connection to the old Viking myths. Since Iceland at this time belonged to Denmark, Brynjólfur donated the manuscript to the Royal Library in Copenhagen, where it gathered dust for several centuries. Only in the nineteenth century, with the chance discovery of an ancient Icelandic manuscript, did interest in Norse mythology bring this material back into popular consciousness. It was, as Tom Shippey says, a dead tradition before then, although he notes that 'Things are very different these days, now that one-eyed Odins, trickster Lokis and hammer-wielding Thors are fantasy and comic-book clichés.'

> Why have these stories broken out of their academic and antiquarian milieu? One secret of their appeal is surely that, in a manner which has always been seen as typically Anglo-Scandinavian, they are deeply gloomy, in a cheerful sort of way. The most striking aspect of Norse mythology is that it is fundamentally hopeless.*

This fundamental hopelessness is important because it grounds the cheerfulness. We can all agree that when disaster looms, despair is a debilitating and counterproductive reaction. What is more contentious is that hope is not much better; it's the hope that generates the anxiety, the tension, that fills you with the terror of uncertainty. It is much better, psychologically as well as practically, to greet the impending disastrousness with a *cheerful hopelessness*. After all: we *are* all doomed.

---

* Tom Shippey, 'Gloomy/Cheerful', *London Review of Books*, 3 January 2008, p. 22.

Everybody dies. There are no exceptions, and it demeans us to deny that fact. The only thing that matters is the courage with which we encounter our inevitable fate.

But then there's one final wrinkle: after all has been lost, there will be a new beginning. The first section of Snorri Sturluson's thirteenth-century *Prose Edda*, the Gylfaginning, contains a detailed account of Ragnarök that moves its story beyond the death of the sun, the devastation of the world, the sea flooding the earth and the sky splitting in two. But 'what comes after the sky and the whole world are burned? After all the gods are dead, and all the world's bravest warriors and the whole of humankind?' The sun's daughter will take her parent's place in the sky; the world will come back to life and two humans whom the gods had hidden away during Ragnarök will emerge: a Norse Adam and Eve called Lif and Lifthrasir. 'They feed on the morning dew,' the Gylfaginning tells us. 'From these so numerous a race is descended that they fill the whole world with people.'

The end turns out not to be the end – Ragnarök turns the universe off and on again. We still can't bring ourselves to come to terms with the total absence of life. Something must continue, something must exist. And so we're locked into a cycle – imagining an end to the story, but afraid to really bring it to an end once and for all. This, counter-intuitively, turns out to be one of the most reliable features of all the stories about the end of the world. A world ends. The world never does.

The Hopi peoples, indigenous to North America and now concentrated in the Hopi Reservation in Arizona, believe that our world is the fourth made by Tawa, their sun spirit creator god. In the first world, things went well initially, but then human beings began to disobey Tawa's laws, becoming violent and sexually promiscuous, and so he brought the world to an end and made another. A different Hopi god, Spider Woman, took pity on the few people who were living virtuous lives but were trapped in the first world. She made a bridge out of a giant hollow reed, and the escapees crossed it into the second world, where the cycle began again. Our fourth world will, we can assume, go the same way,* and we can imagine this process happening over and over again. The end of the world becomes not a finality, but a repeating reiteration.

---

* The question of what will happen in this fourth world is complicated by the question of whether the Hopi conceptualise past, present and future in the ways we do. It used to be thought the Hopi language was tenseless, which would put the concept of a future end of the world in question; the consensus now is that they do have tenses, although the matter is still being debated.

This is, in fact, a feature of the single most influential version of the end of the world ever written: Revelation. Its author was a man who called himself Yohannon but who, as a first-century Greek-speaking Jew, transliterated his name as Ἰωάννης (*Iōánnēs*). English has further morphed this name into John.

The Revelation of St John is the last book in the canonical Bible. It relates a series of bizarre visions of what the end of the world will look like, and it is the most famous 'end of the world' there has ever been. Fanatics and believers still pore over its details, while the popular culture we all consume still has a fascination with this potent vision of the apocalypse. It is manifestly present in modern works as different from one another as Stephen King's enormous novel *The Stand* (1978) and Genesis's lengthy prog-rock song 'Supper's Ready' (1972), as different as the portentous Omen movie series (1976–91) and Terry Pratchett and Neil Gaiman's masterly comic pastiche *Good Omens* (1990). All have fictionalised John's particularities by updating and recontextualising them. Victorian painter John Martin created gigantic canvases illustrating scenes from Revelation that have directly influenced the work of cinematic special-effects artists to this day in the scope and detail of their representations of disaster.

This is the way the world ends: not with a whimper but a bang.

'Revelation' is the standard translation of the book's first word: Ἀποκάλυψις, 'Apocalypse', a word that originally meant 'unveiling', because St John was removing the sheet that veiled the future from us. Perhaps a more up-to-date translation of the word apocalypse would be 'striptease': the story certainly takes its time, building up the tension, as it works through its layers of titillating horror. In the video for Robbie Williams's 2000 single 'Rock DJ', the singer performs a striptease before an audience of adoring women, first taking off his clothes, then his skin and finally his flesh, leaving his skeleton dancing and cavorting. That is the kind of striptease that you will be signing up for if you step inside John's 'apocalypse' nightclub.

The bare bones of John's narrative are worth laying out in a little more detail, both because they have been so influential on later versions of the end of the world and simply because it shows just how drawn out this ending is.

Firstly, John sees a vision of the throne of God, with twenty-four smaller thrones arranged around it. A magic scroll is presented before the big throne. It is sealed with seven wax seals, and the opening of each one is accompanied by a different horrific eventuality that is indicative of the end times. When the first seal is opened, a white horse appears, with the second a red horse, followed by a black horse and finally a pale horse ridden by Death and followed by Hell – the infamous 'four horsemen of the apocalypse'. The fifth seal reveals the souls of those who had been martyred for the word of God, and the sixth seal unleashes a big-budget end-of-the-world spectacular:

> There was a great earthquake; and the sun became black as sackcloth of hair, and the moon became as blood; and the stars of heaven fell unto the earth, even as a fig tree casteth her untimely figs, when she is shaken of a mighty wind. And the heaven departed as a scroll when it is rolled together; and every mountain and island were moved out of their places. And the kings of the earth, and the great men, and the rich men, and the chief captains, and the mighty men, and every bondman, and every free man, hid themselves in the dens and in the rocks of the mountains; and said to the mountains and rocks, 'Fall on us, and hide us from the face of him that sitteth on the throne, and from the wrath of the

Lamb: For the great day of his wrath is come; and who shall be able to stand?'*

The events that follow the opening of the sixth seal look pretty comprehensively like the end of the world, but we are only just getting started. The seventh seal discloses seven trumpets, and the sounding of each unleashes a whole new series of terrible world-ending catastrophes: burning hail falls and destroys one-third of the earth's vegetation; then a flaming mountain falls from the sky, lands in the ocean and destroys one-third of all marine life; the star called Wormwood falls to earth, poisoning the rivers; sunlight, moonlight and starlight lose one-third of their light; a falling meteor opens a smoking abyss in the earth, from which monstrous locust–scorpion hybrids that are shaped like men and wearing iron breastplates swarm. Then four angels that were previously imprisoned in the Euphrates river are released, summoning an army 200 million strong and killing a third of mankind with fire and poisonous gas. The world, says John, is now under the control of the entity that he calls 'the Beast'.

---

* Revelation 6:12–17.

Just as the seventh seal opened to reveal seven trumpets, each one heralding a further horror, so the seventh trumpet announces the arrival of a new set of seven harbingers of disaster, contained in bowls, although the Greek (*phialas*) could also be translated as 'vials'. The contents are not pleasant. The first causes blistering sores on everybody's skin; the second completely poisons the sea; the third turns the rivers to blood; the fourth brings drought; the fifth a choking fog that darkens the whole world; and the sixth dries up the Euphrates and initiates the 'Battle of Armageddon'.

After the seven seals and the seven trumpets, we empty the last of the seven little bottles and finally reach the world's *coup de grâce*. The whole earth convulses and the sky collapses in great chunks, each fragment weighing a talent – about 25 kilograms in modern terms. Every island sinks into the sea and every mountain collapses – the world is dead.

But I spoke too soon, because John's vision continues and so does the world – although how anyone has survived the previous blizzard of world-ending disasters is something of a puzzle. A great city, personified as a sexually promiscuous woman saddled on a gigantic monster, is destroyed. God and the Beast continue to battle; a dragon is released, and once again there is a world-ending war, and another defeat for the Beast. Finally, John sees the replacement of the old heaven and the old earth with a new heaven and earth in which there is no more suffering, death or sin, and where God lives with humanity forever. Phew!

There has been more interpretation of Revelation than all the other books of the Bible put together. I do not propose to add to that great heap, but there are a few things worth drawing out of this account.

The context in which Revelation was written is crucial to our understanding of it. It was created at a time when Christianity was a sect of Judaism, and John was a Jew who believed that Christ was the messiah promised by Jewish scriptures. He may or may not have believed that Christ also came to non-Jews, but it was the fate of his fellow Jews that concerned John most closely.

There's nothing else like Revelation in the New Testament or in the Apocrypha, and while it's true that much of the specific detail of John's vision tends to strike us today as bizarre or incomprehensible, it makes more sense in the context of Jewish prophetic writing, a discourse that has its own symbolic idiom. In the words of the Bible scholar Géza Vermes, 'Revelation, unlike the Gospel, is a typical Jewish apocalypse in which a belligerent Christ, wearing the warrior's bloodstained robe, exterminates all the enemies of God before being transformed into a heavenly bridegroom.'* But even the old Hebrew prophets, though they do sometimes pronounce doom on us miserable sinners, don't lay out the intricate specificity of details about the end of the world in the way that John does. That hadn't been the Jewish way before, but by the time he came to write his book towards the end of the first century, something profound had changed in the world of the Jews.

In 66 CE the Jewish people staged a prolonged and bloody uprising against Roman rule and the Romans spent the next few years brutally suppressing it. The general in charge, Vespasian, crushed Jewish resistance in the north of Judea and then marched south to lay siege to Jerusalem, where he left the army under the command of his son, Titus. After a seven-month siege, Titus finally broke through Jerusalem's city walls, the occupants of which were all either killed or enslaved, and most of the city was burnt or torn down. Most terrible of all, so far as the Jews were concerned, Titus broke into the inner sanctum of Judaism: he marched his soldiers through the seven entrances of the great

---

* Géza Vermes, *Christian Beginnings from Nazareth to Nicaea, AD 30–325* (Penguin, 2012), p. 116.

Temple, the heart of Jewish religious praxis, and tore it down.

Jews today still mourn this disaster. The only piece of the temple still standing, a small fragment of the Western Wall, is a place of pilgrimage to modern Jews, known as the Wailing Wall on account of the public lamentation devout Jews make at that place. Before 70 CE, the Jews lived in Judea, centred around their great Temple in Jerusalem, which was presided over by a high priest. After 70 CE the Jews became a diasporic people scattered all over the world among hostile nations, in an environment poisoned by defeat, oppression and prejudice, setting up synagogues wherever they happened to be staying, with their religious life tended by rabbis, or 'teachers', rather than priests. I am always struck by the way that Passover, the most important religious ritual in Judaism, ends with the claim, pitched somewhere between yearning and that blithe invocation of impossibility that characterises human resilience, that wherever we celebrate this year, *next* year we will celebrate in Jerusalem.

It was in the immediate aftermath of this catastrophe that John wrote his apocalypse. In fact, the word 'armageddon' has a grand and global sound to it, although John's usage was more parochial: 'ar' means hill and 'Megiddo' is a town in northern Israel, once important as a walled city guarding the trade routes from Egypt to Syria and Turkey. Therefore armageddon means 'the battle of Megiddo hill'. While John talks about the whole world, he is fixated on a small stretch of land: modern-day Israel, going no further south than Jerusalem, no further north than the Euphrates (which rises in Turkey and flows through Syria), no further east than Babylon (near modern-day Baghdad) and no further west than Rome. We have taken John's localised world's end and turned it into a cosmic drama, just as we do with our individual mortalities: magnifying them into a collective disaster.

So, by the time John was writing his book, the world had already suffered its terminal catastrophe, and he was writing in the ruins of the disaster. Something integral to Jewish religious practice had been destroyed, never to return. And though it wasn't the end of absolutely everything, it certainly felt like it was to a dispossessed Jew and a persecuted follower of the self-declared Jewish messiah Jesus Christ. The coming of the messiah was supposed to signal the end of times, but instead Christ was crucified and history had rolled on. What could it mean? The Gospels record Christ's own declaration that people with whom he was talking would still be alive when the world ended (Matthew 16:28 and Luke 9:27, for instance). Then, a quarter-century later, the world of the Jews *did* end.

John writes that disaster and affliction had come upon the world, and more specifically upon the bit of the world that really matters, the bit that has a particular covenant with God. He writes that this world had been destroyed by a series of astonishing horrors, but that it still, somehow, continues. He writes that the world ends in fire, just as Jerusalem was burnt; that the mountains of the world collapsed to rubble, just as the Temple was shattered; that disaster rains down from the sky – one of the main legionary forces that wrecked Judea was the 'Thunderbolt Twelfth' and that terrible monsters, shaped like men wearing iron breastplates, ruined the land.

Revelation deliberately hides specific Roman references behind codes and hints. There was a good reason for this: direct attacks on Roman authority might invite sanctions, up to and including crucifixion. For example, by styling the invading Roman legionaries as 'locust–scorpion' hybrids, John was stressing their monstrosity; but combine locusts with scorpions and we also have a flying insect with a sharp sting – a wasp. The cognomen *vespasianus* means 'the waspy one'; both Vespasian and

Titus were surnamed 'the Wasp'. We can imagine John writing that 'the Wasp's people' had come to plague his country, before deciding that was a little too close to the bone and so disguising the wasps as 'locust–scorpions'.

John's 'Beast' doesn't have a name, but he does have a designator: 666 – the 'number of the Beast', the number most associated with the end of the world. This too is likely to be a code. In Greece at the time, numbers were notated using letters (Arabic numerals didn't arrive in Europe until the Middle Ages). The chart below shows which letter corresponded to which number.

α′	1	ι′	10	ρ′	100	͵α	1,000
β′	2	κ′	20	σ′	200	͵β	2,000
γ′	3	λ′	30	τ′	300	͵γ	3,000
δ′	4	μ′	40	υ′	400	͵δ	4,000
ε′	5	ν′	50	φ′	500	͵ε	5,000
ς′	6	ξ′	60	χ′	600	͵ς	6,000
ζ′	7	ο′	70	ψ′	700	͵ζ	7,000
η′	8	π′	80	ω′	800	͵η	8,000
θ′	9	ϙ′	90	ϡ′	900	͵θ	9,000

In the first century CE, it was common to add up the numerical values of the letters of a person's name to get a number to represent that person. 'Isopsephy' – to use the splendidly tongue-twistery technical term

– was very common at the time. Graffiti scrawled on the walls at Pompeii from that time often plays these games: 'I love her whose number is 545'; 'Amerimnus pondered well his lady Harmonia. The number of her honourable name is 45.' It's a fun game,* if you want to keep a name hidden, for erotic reasons – or indeed for reasons of political expediency.

So whose name is encoded in 666? Most scholars think it refers to Nero, who was Roman emperor when the Jewish rebellion began. But Nero died before Jerusalem fell, and it was not he who destroyed the Temple. I think it is more likely that 666 is Titus, the Roman general who ended the world of the Jews when he sacked Jerusalem and tore down the Temple. Titus afterwards became emperor himself. Indeed, if John wrote Revelation in 79, 80 or 81 CE – perfectly possible dates for its composition – he was writing when Titus *was* Caesar.

My larger point is that John is describing something simultaneously local, specific and historical, and something universal, general and spiritual. He is doing so

* My own name, Ἀδάμ, sums to forty-six, which I'll be honest strikes me as a little disappointing (I don't even stretch to a half-century!).

because for him Jerusalem is both an earthly city *and* a spiritual actualisation of God in the world. It's for that reason that Revelation has such a jarring psychedelic oddness to it: what we are looking at are two images superposed one over the other. John of Patmos treated a localised disaster as having a cosmic as well as a local significance. How could it not, for a Jew in 80 CE?

To be clear: I'm not suggesting that John of Patmos wrote a historical account of the fall of Jerusalem rather than a prophetic account of the end of the world. Revelation is, manifestly, the latter and not the former. After all, if John had wanted to write a historical narrative he could have done so, just as his fellow Greek-speaking Jew Josephus did, without any surreal and symbolic bizarreness. John is certainly writing a prophetic account of the end of the world – it's just that he is using a historical event as the prototype for that coming end. For John, Jerusalem was the heart of the world and its destruction enacts, in all its particulars, the coming destruction of the world.

I've discussed John's Revelation at length partly because it has proved so influential on the way art and literature imagine Armageddon, and because my reading of it draws out the ideas I consider important about how we conceptualise the world's end: the idea that it

happens not once, but over and over again, each resulting in a new beginning; and that the grand statements
of apocalypse all relate back to something parochial.

But it's also important because of the way this story
has been interpreted and, in some cases, affected real-
world events. People have looked for a reflection of the
book's symbols in the world around them to predict
the real end of times.

In 1000 CE, the reign of the English king Ethelred
was paralysed not so much by the ongoing Viking raids
on his kingdom as by the warnings of his clergy, most
prominently Wulfstan, the Bishop of London, that these
raids should be welcomed in order that the millennial
apocalypse could be fulfilled. The belief that John's
millennium was coming true crippled Ethelred's ability to defend his kingdom. Various popes, political
leaders and VIPs have been proposed for the role of
John's Beast: Pierre Bezukhov, the hero of Tolstoy's
War and Peace (1869), becomes obsessed by a theory
that Napoleon Bonaparte is the beast, and tries to make
the French emperor's name fit the number it was designated: 666. After the Chernobyl disaster in 1986,
that dreadful explosion at a Ukrainian nuclear reactor,
Revelation-literalists became very excited by the fact
that the variety of wormwood scientifically known as

Artemisia vulgaris is called 'Chernobyl' in Russian – despite the fact the disaster did not poison all the rivers in the world and although a nuclear reactor is hardly a star that can fall from the sky.

In some ways it is understandable: there is an ornate fretwork of bizarre details but they all come down to superficial changes on two fundamental themes running throughout the story. One is what we might call 'environmental disaster': fire and poison falling from the sky, the dying back of vegetation, drought and the contamination of the oceans. The other is political: evil rulers oppress the ordinary people of the world, and soldiers invade the land. Famine and natural disaster are made much worse by war, massacre and destruction. Take away the fanciful grotesqueries in which John's imagination clothes his account and we have something not just familiar but perennial.

And so, as the influence of Revelation spread and the context in which it was written became obscured, people reinterpreted it in terms of their own situations. If you were English in 1000 CE, Viking raids, political instability and the imminence of the very millennium John mentions would have convinced you that the world is ending. If you were an American evangelical in the 1980s who had just discovered that the Russian for wormwood is Chernobyl, then you might convince yourself that the world is ending. It's possible that you are finding yourself struck by elements in the world today that seem to match moments in John's potent book – oceanic dieback, acid falling as rain, myriad environmental pollutions and ongoing war. If you are, you're doing exactly what Revelation invites you to do: stepping from the personalised local to the generalised cosmic and back again. That is natural, because cosmic apocalypse always has an impact on our individual situation. Any death ends the world of that one person; this specificity is inevitable – it's just not important. And at the risk of sounding paradoxical, the fact that it is not important is where its importance lies. We're all ordinary, but this extraordinary thing will happen to each of us: we will die. St John returns again and again to the horror of this, until a magic door opens for a chosen few and they step through into a new heaven and a new earth.

2

A SWARM OF UNDEAD:
THE ZOMBIE APOCALYPSE

You are one of the last human beings left alive. You've hidden for as long as your supplies lasted, but now you must venture outside to find more, or starve. You should tread carefully, because in every street, shambling across every garden, their flesh rank and yet still moving inexorably on, are zombies, hordes of zombies, everywhere, and all of them have only one thing on their mind: to get to you, tear you to pieces and devour you as they come shambling towards you, their flesh rotting and their eyes blank.

It's the premise of thousands of books and films, a scenario so common as to approach cliché. St John's was the dominant vision of apocalypse for generations, but the zombie apocalypse is now more familiar. This is the way the world ends now – not with a bang, but with a monster.

Halfway between religion and science are those myths in which we don't actually believe but that shape our lives anyway. Most people don't believe in ghosts, vampires and zombies, and yet these stories are everywhere in our culture. None, however, have figured quite so prominently in end-of-the-world scenarios as zombies. From George A. Romero's *Night of the Living Dead* (1968) to the big-budget Hollywood movie *World War Z* (2013), zombies have become a screen phenomenon. There are even books that offer readers advice on how to survive any future zombie apocalypse.* These tend to combine a jaunty tongue-in-cheek tone with practical advice, combining a wry sense that it's not serious with the material information we would need if it were.

---

* Over the last decade alone we've seen Bud Hanzel and John Olson's *The Do-It-Yourself Guide to Surviving the Zombie Apocalypse* (2010), Max Brallier's *Can You Survive the Zombie Apocalypse?* (2011) and Bryan Hall's *An Ethical Guidebook to the Zombie Apocalypse: How to Keep Your Brain Without Losing Your Heart* (2019).

It's a striking combination of qualities, as if we neither want to believe in these monsters nor altogether want to sacrifice our belief in them.

Why is it that zombies have become one of the most popular portrayals of the end, more so than any other monster? Partly perhaps because the zombie genre is so versatile; its themes of death, decay, mass-destruction and loss of control can be a useful metaphor for many things. Clearly they speak to our anxieties about death, both as individuals and as a species, but their reanimated corpses can also point to fears of cannibalism, the supersession of thought by empty craving, brainwashing, speechlessness and the herd instinct, to name a few.

So while the 'zombie' trope has become somewhat ubiquitous, there are plenty of examples of writers and directors using the zombie to brilliant and unique effect – although in fear of provoking a 'whatever'-shrug of world-weary readers resistant to cliché they often steer clear of the Z-word itself. So it is that *The Walking Dead* (2003–19), a series of graphic novels written by Robert Kirkman and illustrated by Tony Moore, and later adapted into a successful TV series, talks not of zombies but of 'walkers'. These gruesome figures provide a constant backdrop of threat and menace to *The Walking Dead*'s post-disaster gritty soap opera;

even when they're not the main focus of the storyline, and the survivors are busy grappling with each other, they're lurking round the edges, almost fading into the background. The walkers could be said to represent our dread of the real world around us; our sense that outside our small circles of life and work the world is a horrible and dangerous place.

Likewise, Justin Cronin's blockbuster trilogy, *The Passage* (2010), *The Twelve* (2012) and *The City of Mirrors* (2016), explores our fears of plague and disease – presciently so for works written before the Covid-19 global lockdown – with his zombie–vampire hybrids as 'virals'. Colson Whitehead's novel *Zone One* (2011), set in a New York overrun with 'skels', uses its premise powerfully to explore the anxieties of contemporary urban America, including immigration. And M. R. Carey's deftly handled novel *The Girl with All the Gifts* (2014) is written from the point of view of an intelligent and self-aware zombie girl, a 'hungry', being studied in a facility. With the characters searching for a cure by any means necessary, including killing and dissecting these almost human-like child zombies, the story thoughtfully explores conflicts between scientific endeavour, ethics and compassion, as well as the struggle for survival and evolution.

Whether cliché or unique, our modern portrayals of the zombie have evolved considerably since its origins as a specifically Haitian, voodoo idea, in which a sorcerer is able to reanimate the dead, but they are fully under his control. As the science fiction writer Charlie Stross* notes: 'The zombie myth has roots in Haitian slave plantations. These stories are fairly transparently about the slaves' fear of being forced to toil endlessly even after their death.'

Shuffling out of the margins of empire, from Haiti and the French Antilles, zombies made the leap from folklore to film in director Victor Halperin's surprise hit *White Zombie* (1932) in which Bela Lugosi plays a mill-owner in Haiti who uses voodoo not only to control his black zombie workers, but to control a beautiful young white woman too – 'With These Zombie Eyes He Rendered Her Powerless,' screamed the posters, over a lurid representation of the creature's stare. 'With This Zombie Grip He Made Her Perform His Every Desire!'

As times and society gradually changed, signalling the end of slavery and of white supremacy, so the idea

---

* . . . while lamenting that the Covid-19 outbreak made it impossible for him to publish a novel that he had been planning in which a fictional virus turns people into zombies . . .

of the zombie changed with it – unleashing them from their masters, and leaving them free to run rampant across the world. As Stross says:

> This narrative got appropriated and transplanted to America, in film, TV and fiction, where it hybridized with white settler fear of a slave uprising. The survivors/protagonists of the zombie plague are the viewpoint the audience is intended to empathize with, but their response to the shambling horde is as brutal and violent as any plantation owner's reaction to their slaves rising, and it speaks to a peculiarly American cognitive disorder, elite panic.*

In its origins, the zombie is undeniably a racialised figure, but in the last half-century its connotations with race have largely disappeared. An echo of the original narrative still exists in its own guise, as concerns regarding racial discrimination in its many forms have not gone away. Particularly in America, the Black Lives Matter protests have spread across the country in response to police brutality and the targeting of

---

* Charlie Stross, 'Yet Another Novel I Will No Longer Write', www.antipope.org, 2 April 2020.

the black population, and this continuing struggle for equality is still discernible in popular culture. *Get Out* (2017) may not have featured the characteristic zombies we have come to recognise today, but in the horrifying kidnapping and brainwashing of its black victims, we can certainly recognise the zombie in its original form, and related fears of domination and oppression.

Nowadays, of course, the word 'zombie' conjures a different picture. The general consensus of their characteristics is that they look like us – ordinary people in dressed-down clothes – but in some state of decay, their flesh rotting, body parts missing, blank-eyed and void of consciousness. In most cases they move with a stumbling, forward shuffle. They are motivated not by rational thought but by hunger to reach us, the living: to devour our brains and to make us like them.

George A. Romero's *Night of the Living Dead* is the movie that set in motion the rise of the zombie as we know it in popular culture. It features the African American actor Duane Jones as protagonist, leading the survivors. This was a bold casting choice by Romero, and works as a deliberate inversion of the racist connotations that Stross identifies. But Romero's many zombie sequels, and the many more films made by other directors, move beyond race as a focus.

As we've seen, in its modern concept that focus can vary considerably, but a consistent theme is disease. The next chapter will consider our fears of disease more closely, but it's clear that zombies have become a vector for contagion – in *28 Days Later* (2002) for example, they are 'the infected', and they sprint towards their victims with terrifying single-mindedness, an unsettling revision of the familiar 'slow zombie' archetype by writer Alex Garland and director Danny Boyle. There is of course one key difference from the spread of a real-life disease: viruses and bacteria are too small to be seen with the naked eye, whereas zombies, whether shuffling or hurtling after you, can hardly be missed. They make manifest, and thus visually interesting, a process that is otherwise invisible and tricky to capture dramatically. They personify plague. And that plague sweeps through the population at an alarming rate, creating the modern-day zombie horde.

That is perhaps why they are more popular than any other monster – this tendency to swarm. Compare them, for example, to another enduring monster that haunts our nightmares: the vampire. It is a popular and recurring figure certainly, but vampire *apocalypse* is hardly a genre in the same way. There's no intrinsic reason why this should be. After all, vampires and zombies both spread their condition by biting, and both are driven by a powerful compulsion to seek out new victims. The combination of these two factors means that both vampires and zombies, were either actually to exist in our world, would quickly lead to apocalypse. In 2008, the University of Central Florida physics professor Costas Efthimiou calculated that if one vampire had bitten one victim each month in 1600, thereby turning them into a vampire, the law of exponentiality means that it would have taken just two and a half years for the entire original human population to become vampires, with nobody left to feed on. If you imagine a greedier vampire, apocalypse arrives even more promptly.*

But, rather than appearing in the context of an apocalypse, in our popular culture vampires tend to live hidden away in small-scale populations, and only come out from time to time to feed on us. Perhaps the difference is that vampires are rational beings and realise that if they infect all the humans they'll exhaust their food supply, and so they restrain themselves? Brian Aldiss's splendidly hokey *Dracula Unbound* (1990) is one of the

* Efthimiou did not calculate the comparative rate for zombies, but as they are considerably less restrained in their feeding habits than vampires, we can assume that global apocalypse would arrive even more swiftly.

few works that portrays what a 'vampire apocalypse' might look like: a dusty world under a weakening sun in the distant future, where the vampires that have conquered the world keep a few humans alive as food. However, this is an exception; vampires are generally marginal figures, while zombies are the means by which the world as we know it ends.

It might not be logical in terms of story, but it is in terms of cultural symbolism. The stereotypical vampire is superior, elegant, suave, sexually promiscuous, well-dressed and well-mannered – until, that is, he bites you. We think about vampires in the same way that we think about aristocracy, which is a small-scale phenomenon, if powerful and often malign. Zombies, by contrast, are not posh or sexy.* Zombies are not aristocrats. Zombies are the masses. Zombies are us. They are the mindless hordes of shopping-mall consumers, brains emptied out by late-stage capitalism and social media. Zombies know nothing except that *they want*, as they shuffle forward (or in latter-day versions, run) at the object of their desire: life. It is about consumption, and the way modernity has infected us all with the virus of consumerism.

* Unless unrelenting mindlessness and rotting flesh are your kinks.

There's a reason why shopping malls and super-markets figure so prominently in zombie apocalypses, and it's not just that such spaces can be cheap filming locations for cash-strapped movie producers. Zombies have come to represent how we think about democra-tisation, consumerisation and globalisation, which are all large-scale mass phenomena. According to the critic Roger Luckhurst:

> The remorseless zombie attack was bedded down as a familiar Gothic trope after Romero's *Dawn of the Dead* (1978) . . . it leaped host again in 1996, when the Japanese computer giant Capcom released the video game *Resident Evil*. Since the late 1990s over twenty different versions of the *Resident Evil* game have been released (along with an associated film franchise). These commodities have made billions of dollars of profit, and have been one of the main vectors ensuring that the zombie has become a truly global figure – arguably the central Gothic figure for globalization itself.*

* Roger Luckhurst, *Zombies: a Cultural History* (Reaktion Books, 2015), pp. 7–8.

Take *Shaun of the Dead* (2004), one of the most successful zombie films of the twenty-first century. It is a
comedy – the common ground that exists between the
physical contortions of slapstick and the conventions of
zombie film-making provide a fertile ground for hilarity. A yell, a blow and a little blood can be sickening,
because it speaks to our real-life experiences of violence;
the elaborate exaggeration of that experience, on the
other hand – a set of operatic screams, overly elaborate
and great gouts of blood and gore – moves us in a different direction. Our response to horror is finely balanced,
and can tip either into terror or into hilarity. This movie
understands how to nudge its reactions consistently in
the latter direction. The sequence in which the film's
three leads, Simon Pegg, Kate Ashfield and Nick Frost,
are trapped in a pub by the zombie hordes outside and
beat one to death with snooker cues in time to the beat
of Queen's 'Don't Stop Me Now' (which is playing on
the pub jukebox) is as hilarious as it is apposite.

But the real comedy of this movie is rooted in its
mundanity, as if the end of the world were not an extraordinary eruption of the spectacular but a repetition
of the everyday. In an early sequence before the zombies arrive, Simon Pegg's Shaun – a lowly electronics
salesman – goes to the corner shop one morning and

returns to his flat, passing shuffling Londoners who are sleepy, hungover or homeless. The sequence is repeated once the zombie apocalypse has started, and Shaun makes the entire trip without even noticing that the sleepy, hungover or destitute Londoners he passes this time are now shuffling, groaning zombies. It is a funny joke, but also something more: it is making a profound statement about how this apocalypse is not a new thing but rather the intensified repetition of the overfamiliar old things in modern life. We're so caught up in its mundanity that we are barely distinguishable from the braindead monsters.

The zombie genre has become, in fact, a reaction against the ubiquity of capitalism; the corruption of our minds leads to the corruption of society as these creatures – us – bring the whole system crashing down. As Michael Newton writes, 'It would appear that we also like to see everything destroyed, Philadelphia overrun by a zombie army, Atlanta's skyscrapers burned-out. Anything seems better than a thousand years of Tescos.'*

---

* Michael Newton, 'The Thrill of It All: Zombies', *London Review of Books*, 18 February 2016, p. 27.

Don't misunderstand me: capitalism has proven itself a powerful machine for generating material wealth (not at distributing that wealth equally, but let's put that to one side), and adding all manner of new products and consumer durables and tech and toys to our lives. But even its most enthusiastic supporters would agree that it has done these things at a cost of social cohesion and harmony. We sometimes focus and rely on these 'things' more than we do on our personal relationships. We force our bodyclocks into the more rigid timetables of work, stumbling zombie-like out of bed in the morning. We live, increasingly, in isolated urban environments, experiencing loneliness, going through the repetitive motions of modern life.

Aldous Huxley's *Brave New World* (1932) is clearly not a zombie novel in the conventional sense, but in this context it absolutely is: in Huxley's hyper-capitalist 'utopia' everybody is (as we would now say) genetically engineered to work, buy things and have sex, to the point where nobody enjoys anything but their work, their shopping and their sex. If people ever feel low, they take a drug called 'soma' to brighten their mood. This is the whole horizon of Huxley's imagined world, and although it is bright and high-tech and its citizens firm-fleshed and good-looking, it reveals itself as a place precisely as soulless, as hunger-driven and as dead as any zombiverse.

In a way the greatest damage capitalism does, as a system, is to prioritise one thing – wealth – over everything else. The pursuit of money supersedes all the values we might say make us human, such as compassion, justice, empathy, honour. The ideal citizen in such a system is driven by an urge to consume, and doesn't think too long and hard, for instance about who's in power or what their agenda is.

And that is, perhaps, the secret core of the zombie story. It is not so much the end of the world, but the end of the values that underpinned that world – not the end of humans as a species, but of our very humanity. In the zombie landscape, the moral decay of society is no longer hidden by the façades of our gleamingly intact cities; it is clear to see in the ruinous cityscapes, in the crumbling remains of our 'civilisations'. The survivors often still try to cling to our traditional social constructs and ideals, banding together in their little communities, helping each other navigate their way through this uncaring, chaotic world. But their attempts to do so are constantly challenged by not only the mindless victims this new order has already claimed but also by other survivors who have enthusiastically embraced the lack of social constraints. The latter are motivated by power and greed, giving in to their baser instincts in the struggle to come out on top. The zombie is not always the biggest monster in these stories; as the critic Eugene Thacker says, 'the unhuman is more likely to reside within the human itself'.*

It is not only the flaws in our capitalist system that might drive us to this point. Zombie outbreaks have become synonymous with many of humanity's self-destructive tendencies, from nuclear holocaust to bioengineering. Mira Grant's 'Parasitology' trilogy – *Parasite* (2013), *Symbiont* (2014) and *Chimera* (2015) – creates a near-future world in which humans carry genetically engineered 'SymboGen' tapeworms in their guts to enable them to combat disease and obesity; but the law of Frankensteinian unintended consequences means that these tapeworms malfunction, become self-aware and escape their hosts' bodies, killing some of them and turning hordes of others into 'sleepwalkers'. In more and more portrayals of the zombie apocalypse, the outbreak is our fault, and

---

* Eugene Thacker, 'Weird, Eerie, and Monstrous: a review of Mark Fisher's *The Weird and the Eerie*', B2o: an Online Journal, June 2017: http://www.boundary2.org/2017/07/

we must accept the consequences. As Xavier Aldana Reyes says:

> Zombies ... increasingly, warn of the end of civilisation that may be precipitated by global crises exacerbated by national economic pressures, such as climate change, or by biological warfare. Contemporary zombie texts mark a significant move away from the moment of outbreak as the focal plot point and toward the long-lasting effects of catastrophes for which humans are directly responsible.*

This may also be why zombie films embody a certain hopelessness over the future. As people and resources dwindle, it becomes clear that there's no going back to their previous way of life. The survivors are just treading water, eking out an existence with no meaning and no real future, alone and abandoned, staring into the face of the inevitable end of humanity. Even if they are able to defeat the plague of the braindead creatures,

---

* Xavier Aldana Reyes, 'Contemporary Zombies', in Maisha Wester and Xavier Aldana Reyes (eds) *Twenty-First-Century Gothic: An Edinburgh Companion* (Edinburgh University Press, 2019), p. 90.

they'll be left to contend with their legacy of a ruined landscape. Max Brooks' *World War Z: An Oral History of the Zombie War* (2006) tells the story of the zombie apocalypse, exploring how the world has been rebuilt and adapted, but few other stories envision this victory or how a new world could be born out of such destruction. It would be a sad thought if our existential loneliness had reached the state where we cannot see past it.

Grief and loneliness are ghastly things: brain-numbing, flesh-corrupting states that bend our lives around the lines of their force. In the French film *The Night Eats the World* (*La nuit a dévoré le monde*, directed by Dominique Rocher, 2018) the main character wakes after a party to find himself utterly alone in the aftermath of a zombie bloodbath. Despite adapting to survive in this new world, his isolation slowly drives him to madness and hallucination.

Groups fare little better: while mourning the loss of humankind, they must also constantly watch helplessly as their own members succumb to the plague, slowly taken over by death. *Maggie* (directed by Henry Hobson, 2015) may not be Arnold Schwarzenegger's best-known movie, but it is one of his more interesting. In the film, a zombie pandemic – called 'necroambulism', another attempt to steer clear of the zombie cliché while embracing its symbolic power – has collapsed society; Arnie's young daughter Maggie is bitten on the arm and Arnie nurses her as she descends into the inevitable zombification. For a while, and despite manifest deterioration (at one point she is woken by maggots wriggling in the dead flesh of her bitten arm), she carries on more-or-less as normal; but there is no cure, and they both know that when Maggie finally 'turns' her father will have to accept her 'death' head on – he will have to kill her. There's real poignancy in this exploration of grief and loss. It speaks to the experiences of so many who have watched their loved ones' lives slowly claimed by unstoppable diseases.

In reminding us of our mortality, zombies also force us to confront our physicality. They record our disgust at our own bodies' senescence and the inevitable decay of our flesh. We are deteriorating even as we speak, transforming our physical appearance long before death takes us. But they also record a more particular terror: that our bodies' decay will continue beyond our deaths.

This is all connected with a unique aspect of our relationship with our own bodies. There are things that we *are* – brave, intelligent, curious, loving, lazy and so on – and then there are things that we *have*, like clothes and books. But the body exists in both these categories, for we both have and *are* our bodies. Our culture's fascination with body horror is one of the ways in which we address the fundamental weirdness of this fault line between having and being. On the one hand our bodies are bestial, disease-prone, decaying flesh that we yearn to escape; on the other, a life lived in the mind would be a barren sort of existence – real life involves inhabiting the real world while being mindful of the sensual richness of embodied experience.*

And while we might primarily think of our minds as being 'us', for many of us our bodies are a fundamental part of that identity, and the idea of leaving it rotting in the ground is not a pleasant one. What happens to our bodies after death has occupied us for millennia. Many of our burial practices are to do with grieving; but they are also to do with concern for what happens to our physical bodies. The Egyptians, for example, believed the body would be important in the next life, hence the process of mummification. In modern times, there are

---

* In the movie *Love and Death* (1975), Woody Allen's Boris sums up the movie in his final monologue: 'The question is: have I learned anything about life? Only that human beings are divided into mind and body. The mind embraces all the nobler aspirations, like poetry and philosophy. But the body has all the fun.'

still processes to preserve the body, while others would rather be cremated than leave their bodies to slowly fester. Zombies perfectly capture the horror we might feel at the prospect of this, as we are forced to confront, in fascinated revulsion, these decomposing corpses outside of the grave.

So horrified are we by the knowledge that our bodies are already on that steady decline to putrefaction that there are people who undertake onerous medical and surgical intervention, and spend prodigious sums, to stamp out the signs of ageing, to project an illusion that their flesh does not and will not decay. We all know how that goes: beyond a certain point, the hysterical denial of our intrinsic fate becomes even more alarming and bizarre than simple acceptance. There is no stopping the ravaging effects of time.

Worse still, perhaps our fascination with zombies comes not from our fear of death but our fear that we *won't* die, that our beings will never escape our bodies and that after our deaths we will neither move on to some spiritual plane nor cease to be, but will carry on, our souls and bodies rotting together – a terrifying idea. This is perhaps connected to the different indignities we might suffer as we age. We might be fully in command of our faculties, but trapped in a body that is deteriorating before our very eyes. Or our bodies are fit and healthy but our minds are slowly being taken over by dementia. Witnessing the gradual but unstoppable slide into the mindlessness of the zombie state is an awful experience suffered in real life by a million carers around the world, as their elderly loved ones succumb to Alzheimer's disease.

In both their mindless and their rotting state, zombies speak to all our fears of what old age holds in store. In the stories we tell, when forced to confront what is happening to the people around them as they turn into unrecognisable creatures, the characters often question whether there is anything left of the original person. In reality, when our minds and our bodies eventually betray us, will we lose what it is to be ourselves?

Zombies are scary not because they are dead and they want us to die too, but because they are trapped in a never-ending state of dying, and they want us to be trapped too, in our decaying and deracinated selves. We may think we want to avoid the inevitable ending, death, but we also yearn for the peace death represents – a natural death, after a natural life, is the last thing of which we should be afraid. It is the inescapable decline of everything in life – the gradual rotting of our bodies, our minds, our societies and even our humanity – that is truly terrifying.

Through their symbolistic versatility, zombies provide a place where many different stories intersect: apocalypse by plague; climate apocalypse; apocalypse by entropy. These decaying corpses have become the focal point for so many of our fears and insecurities that they have become the ultimate expression for the end of the world.

3

BRING OUT YOUR DEAD: WORLD-ENDING PLAGUES

In Homer's *Iliad*, set in the twelfth century BCE, the Greek army laying siege to Troy unwisely disrespects one of Apollo's priests. In response, the god shows his displeasure by firing his arrows of contagion into their camp: 'the mules he assailed first and the swift dogs, but then he let fly his stinging shafts on the men themselves, and struck; and constantly the pyres of the dead burned thick'. The plague lasts for nine days – brief by modern standards. After the Greeks make amends to the priest and sacrifice sheep and goats to Apollo, the plague is cured.

Seven centuries later, a real-life plague struck Athens, killing a quarter of the city's population and setting the city state on a path to military defeat at the hands of Sparta. Greeks of the time had a simple explanation for the pandemic: Apollo. The Spartans had supplicated to the god, and he had promised them victory; soon afterwards, their enemies started dying of the plague. Hindsight suggests that Athens was under siege and its population swollen with refugees; as a result, everyone was living in unsanitary conditions and at risk of contagion in a way that the Spartan army, free to roam the countryside outside, was not. However, this thought didn't occur to the Ancient Greeks and they blamed the god.

Stories of plague-driven apocalypse abound, in movies such as *Outbreak* (1995) and *Contagion* (2011), but unlike the gods and monsters of our previous chapters, disease has always been a very real feature in human life, as well as in our stories. We understand contagion vastly better now, and have a greater arsenal of medicine and hygiene to fight it, but we are all susceptible still. This is both a bad and a good thing: bad because disease can cripple or kill; but good because our bodies respond to disease by developing antibodies. Every parent knows that the seemingly endless parade of snotty noses and various lurgies that define their kids' early years are necessary for those kids to build healthy immune systems, however distressing the process can be for all concerned.

What is true on an individual level is also true on a civilisational level; and just as the body sometimes succumbs to disease, so whole communities can be – and have been – devastated. In his influential study *Guns, Germs, and Steel* (1997), Jared Diamond considers the defining role disease has played in human history. In Europe, argues Diamond, because people moved around extensively, to trade for example, disease spread easily between different regions. This looks like a bad thing, and it's true that a series of ghastly plagues afflicted medieval and Renaissance Europe: 75 million Europeans died of the Black Death in the fourteenth century – almost half the entire population of the continent. But there was a hard-won advantage: the survivors of these plagues carried antibodies to the germs that caused them.

When Europeans began spreading around the world they were able to use their superior technology and weapons of war to conquer other continents. But even more importantly for the trajectory of human history, these Europeans brought with them diseases to which populations in other parts of the globe had no immunity. European settlers in North America and Australia killed vastly greater numbers of natives with their diseases than with their guns. Chickenpox and measles, which Europeans might survive, tended to be deadly to such populations, and resulted in human suffering and death on a staggering scale.

This was the point in history where disease moved from being a local affliction to being a way in which the world ends. Many epidemics have had a catastrophic effect on populations. The Wampanoag population of Native Americans, mostly located in modern-day New England, suffered up to 90 per cent loss of population as a European disease, now thought to be leptospirosis, spread through their tribes. In the cocoliztli epidemic of 1545–48, in what is now Mexico, 12 million people – a staggering 80 per cent of the native population – died of a disease brought by European settlers that was either a variant smallpox or a gastroenteritic sickness. A further two and a half million people, half the remaining population, died in a second outbreak of the sickness in 1576. In 1803, prior to British colonisation, the island of 'Van Diemen's Land', modern-day Tasmania, had a population of roughly 10,000 native Palawa, but by 1847 European disease and murder had reduced this population to fewer than fifty people. Aspects of their heredity have survived in Australia to the present day, but the last person of solely native Tasmanian descent died in 1905. These are figures that numb the brain with the sheer scale of their horror.

That said, and without ignoring the ghastliness of these cases, disease never wipes out literally everyone on its own. Even in the case of the Palawans it required war, killing, starvation and colonial oppression to finish that terrible job. The biggest epidemic of the twentieth century was Spanish flu in 1918–20. As many as 100 million people died globally; but grievous though this certainly was, it represented less than 5 per cent of the world's population. I don't mean to sound dismissive, because of course 100 million is a horrific and devastating figure, but it didn't come anywhere near ending the world.

In reality, the risk that the white horseman of Revelation, wielding his deadly plague, will destroy the whole world has been receding for a long time. As the global population increases, and as globalisation mixes up populations, epidemics have less bite, thanks to a better understanding of how to prevent the spread of disease, and the twinned healthcare countermeasures of immunisation and the improved treatment of those who fall sick. But the *perceived* risk keeps rising, because we are more aware of the specificities of disease and how devastating they can be. Global life is interconnected nowadays to an unprecedented degree, and 'interconnectedness' is a shorthand for 'possible pathways of contagion'. Popular culture and contemporary social commentary are subject to repeated bouts of 'pandemic anxiety'. The BBC TV show *Survivors* (1975–77) vividly realised this in its opening credits: one man, infected with a terrible new plague but as yet unaware, is shown flying from airport to airport, getting his passport stamped. The actual show, set after the plague had killed 4,999 out of every 5,000 people, dealt with the consequences. The virus in that show was fictional, but the hit 1995 movie *Outbreak* imagined an Ebola-like virus spreading from Africa to America. The movie perks up its storyline with fights, chases, military conspiracies to develop the virus as a bioweapon and a plan to bomb an American town to contain it, to melodramatic effect; but it opens with real-life molecular biologist and Nobel laureate Joshua Lederberg informing the audience: 'the single biggest threat to man's continued dominance on the planet is the virus'.

These fictions inform our reality. Fear of H5N1 avian flu caused widespread panic in the early 2000s, and the mere prospect of an outbreak of Ebola or the Zika virus terrifies us today. Sometimes those fears prove grounded – as we all found out with the outbreak of Covid-19. But despite the global disruption and the devastation caused by individual fatalities, it was not heralding the apocalypse. Of course it makes sense to take precautions where any disease is concerned, but panic and overreaction is neither sensible nor precautionary.

My point is that disease plays an actual as well as a fantastical role in our lives, and it is the latter that is often apocalyptic. While the individual experience of disease can be horrible and may be fatal, it is in the nature of apocalyptic imagining to extrapolate individuality onto the global canvas.

Besides the scale of imagined devastation, the other fictional element we ascribe to our pandemics is *agency* – a sense that they have purpose, that they are not merely random. When the Peloponnesian plague targeted only Athenians, contemporaries concluded that the gods were angry with Athens, and when HIV first appeared in gay communities, some concluded that God was angry with homosexuals. Neither statement was true; HIV spreads wherever it can and doesn't care about your sexual orientation. Nonetheless, when it comes to our suffering, we want it to *mean* something. We dislike arbitrariness. We want to understand *why* it's happening, so we can fix it, or try to, but also for the less rational reasons that we prefer an enemy with a face to a faceless one. We want to feel we can fight back, even if the fight is impossible, like homeowners shooting their guns at the hurricane they know is rolling in to destroy their houses. We can see this desire to assign 'agency' to the virus in those who insist that the coronavirus is a Chinese experimental bioweapon gone rogue, or supporters of Donald Trump who see a shadowy conspiracy of 'deep state' actors happy to sacrifice millions of lives in a plot to scupper their president's re-election prospects. To them, even malign actors are more reassuring than blind happenstance; angry gods are better than no gods at all.

However, it is not true – disease has no agency. Bacteria and viruses spread wherever they can, their paths facilitated by our massively globalised world, and we bring our ever-improving drugs and hygiene to the struggle. One lesson we have all learned from the coronavirus pandemic, repeated over and over again by the experts, is that the best advice is to wash your hands often, avoid touching your face and keep as much distance between yourself and others as possible. But people do not warm to the arbitrary nature of this. People prefer a plan. 'You know what I've noticed?' says the Joker in Christopher Nolan's *Dark Knight* (2008). 'Nobody panics when things go "according to plan" . . . even if the plan is horrifying.' It doesn't reflect very well on us, but it's true. Because what's the alternative? A Jokerish anarchy?

This need to attribute agency to the disease is clearest in the many plagues that writers of science fiction have inflicted on humanity. In Alice Sheldon's chilling and brilliant short story 'The Screwfly Solution' (1977) a new disease provokes men to murder women en masse. At the end of the story we discover that an alien species had introduced a brain infection to make the human race destroy itself, so they can inherit the planet – apocalypse by targeted disease. In H. P. Lovecraft's *The Colour Out of Space* (1927) an alien infection arrives via a meteorite and drives people mad. In other stories the world-threatening plague has been caused by that other science fiction stalwart: the 'mad scientist'. The scientist in the movie *The Satan Bug* (1965), having inoculated himself, hopes that the rest of the world will die of his germ, for reasons of environmental fundamentalism. In Frank Herbert's novel *The White Plague* (1982) a geneticist who has been driven to insanity by the murder of his family creates a pathogen that kills only females. On the other side of the gender divide is Joanna Russ's feminist masterpiece, *The Female Man* (1975), where in one of the alternative versions of earth's future it portrays, a gender-specific virus has wiped out the men. By the novel's end it is hinted that the man-destroying plague was engineered by a female scientist irked by the patriarchy. Likewise, dozens of zombie franchises start with a rogue scientist infecting the population with a genetically engineered virus.

So characteristic is assigning agency to pandemics in modern culture that the video game *Plague Inc.* (2012) styles its players not as doctors who are attempting to stop the spread of a pandemic, but as the sickness itself. The player's mission is to help their plagues spread and exterminate the human race. The game's algorithm uses a complex and realistic set of variables to simulate the spread of the plague, and models a convincing version of today's interconnected globe. If you make your sickness too virulent, people will die before it can be passed on; if you make it too mild, people will develop resistance or medical science will create a rendered with all the melodramatic dash and special effects that modern film-making can bring to bear. The crucial thing about the plague here is that *it wears our face*. We are disease. What is wrecking the planet, while bubonic plague, smallpox, typhus, Spanish flu and AIDS do nothing more than eat away at the edge of our continuing expansion, is our population itself.

The way we portray disease in our stories is always changing as our societies grapple with the different diseases that afflict them, and their after-effects. Boccaccio's *Decameron* (1353), the celebrated medieval collection of stories, is a plague book – its tales were assembled as diversions for quarantined nobles during the Black Death – but its emphasis is resolutely *not* on the disease itself. The stories it collects are overwhelmingly light-hearted, satirical *contes*, comic tales and love stories, intermixed with the occasional tragedy. This conceivably reflects the fact that the Black Death was so horrible that the last thing people wanted was to be reminded of it. Hans Holbein's famous *Danse Macabre* woodcuts from the early sixteenth century are grisly, but they are also witty and even hilarious. Across dozens of woodcuts, Holbein portrays death as a grinning skeleton interrupting all manner of people in the middle of their day-to-day lives: a ploughman,

cure. The game has sold over 85 million copies, which suggests there are plenty of people interested in adding smallpox to *The Sims* or introducing syphilis into Sid Meier's *Civilization*.

Another twist in a slew of science fiction tales, from H. G. Wells's seminal *The War of the Worlds* (1898) through to various modern retellings such as *Independence Day*, is that the virus is on our side, destroying alien invaders that lack our acquired immunity.

Perhaps the best portrayal of this conceit is Greg Bear's *Blood Music* (1985). A mad scientist, angry at being sacked from his job, smuggles an experimental virus out of his lab. It infects everybody, becomes self-aware and then assimilates everybody to itself: not only human beings but their houses, cities and landscapes melt down into a planet-wide sea of hyperintelligent grey goo. It sounds unpleasant, but it is actually a liberation: the accumulation of concentrated consciousness causes a transcendent new realm. Bear's plague is responsible for a kind of secular Rapture.

Is it odd that we sometimes take the side of the pandemic in our storytelling? Maybe not. The theory of the contagion being God's anger implies that we are guilty and deserve what we are getting. When Rick Jaffa and Amanda Silver reinvigorated the *Planet of the Apes* franchise, they assumed that the same agent that raises the apes' level of intelligence, a neuro-enhancing compound spliced into simian flu, would prove fatal to humans. The resulting trilogy (2011–17) was more than just a commercial hit; it was also an eloquent, if sometimes rather unsubtle, articulation of environmental anxiety. The few surviving humans on the planet move through the movies' lush forestscapes, encountering newly intelligent apes who have become avatars of humanity's contempt for the natural world. The plague that has destroyed us has given these animals wisdom, and they are angry with us. Hard to blame them, really.

Our fascination with plague has something to do with our fear that we are the offenders and that these diseases are furies that have been aroused by our guilt. Think of the artificial intelligence Mr Smith in *The Matrix* (1999), played with sneering panache by Hugo Weaving. Humans, he tells Laurence Fishburne's Morpheus, are incapable of developing a natural equilibrium with their environment:

> You move to an area and you multiply and multiply until every natural resource is consumed and the only way you can survive is to spread to another area. There is another organism on this planet that follows the same pattern. Do you know what it is? A virus. Human beings are a disease, a cancer of this planet. You're a plague and we are the cure.

The third Matrix film contains my favourite scene, what to me is a visually inventive and extraordinarily eloquent critique on the subject of plague within the story of machines. Inside the Matrix, Smith has copied himself over every other human being alive. The world's cities throng with reduplicated Smiths wearing black suits and dark glasses, glowering malevolently and preparing to destroy Neo, who walks down a storm-lashed street past ranks upon ranks of Smiths. Everybody is Smith now, evil and destructive, and Neo's fight with one of these myriad Smiths, on the ground, in the air, through buildings and finally into a terminal crater in which his inevitable defeat is enacted, is wonderful cinema. The two men fight like gods and Neo is cast down. 'This is my world!' yells a gloating Smith as he hovers in the sky with lightning bolts behind him – and he's right.

As a visual representation of the way in which the spreading of plague symbolises the proliferation of the human race, I don't believe these scenes have been bettered. This is world-ending disease personified, and

an abbot, a fine lady prettifying herself, a pedlar, a king. It's ghastly, but the look of astonishment – the 'who? *me?*'-ness of it all – is grimly comic too.

The plagues of modernity, while still awful (TB, cholera, typhus and typhoid killed hundreds of millions across nineteenth-century Europe), are more diluted by a larger population and less concentrated in specific bursts. Perhaps that is why we see such a shift in tone from the comic and light-hearted to the gothic and ghastly of the nineteenth century, encapsulated perfectly by some of the stories that writers Byron, Shelley, Polidori and Mary Godwin (who later became Mary Shelley) came up with while socially isolating in the Villa Diodati in Switzerland in 1816.

Mary Shelley's novel *The Last Man* (1826), for example, is ponderously gloomy, its dramatis personae all poseurs, its plotting an improbable mixture of aristo soap opera and war. The story is set in a late-twenty-first-century England more or less indistinguishable from England in 1800. Shelley's three main characters are cyphers for herself and her friends: Lionel Verney, the eponymous Last Man, is a gender-swapped Mary; Adrian, Earl of Windsor (son of the last king of England) is Percy Bysshe Shelley; and the charismatic and passionate young nobleman Lord Raymond (who becomes

Lord Protector of England, as the plague continues to cull the population) is Lord Byron. As the population thins, Verney and his friends flee Britain in the hope of escaping contagion. This is a vain hope: they die on the way or drown in a shipwreck, except Verney, who swims ashore at Ravenna with the knowledge that he is the last human being alive. The novel ends with him walking to Rome, his only company a sheepdog he picks up on the way. There he contemplates spending the rest of his life roaming the now empty world:

> A solitary being is by instinct a wanderer, and that I would become. A hope of amelioration always attends on change of place, which would even lighten the burthen of my life . . . Tiber, the road which is spread by nature's own hand, threading her continent, was at my feet, and many a boat was tethered to the banks. I would with a few books, provisions and my dog embark in one of these and float down the current of the stream into the sea; and then, keeping near land, I would coast the beauteous shores and sunny promontories of the blue Mediterranean . . . Thus around the shores of deserted earth, while the sun is high, and the moon waxes or wanes, angels, the spirits of

the dead, and the ever-open eye of the Supreme, will behold the tiny bark, freighted with Verney – the LAST MAN.

There were a great many 'last man' poems and stories at the start of the nineteenth century; far from initiating it, Shelley's novel chased the coat-tails of this trend. Frenchman Jean-Baptiste de Grainville's *Dernier Homme* (1805) was the prototype for this particular mode, and since then there have been hundreds of examples. You might think stories of everybody dying of the plague would be examples of tragedy, either gloomily or stoically encountered, but in fact these stories usually inhabit the more complicated heady elegiacism of *freedom,* albeit one purchased at a heavy price. Part of the appeal of this kind of story is its peculiar blend of melancholy exhilaration. The deal here is the thrill of a guilt-struck but liberated loneliness: tragic finality combined with all sorts of possibilities, the whole world our oyster, unrestricted by other people.

Freud talked of civilisation *and* its discontents* – arguing that the cost of living in a civilised society is the

---

* He did so in a book called, appropriately enough, *Civilization and its Discontents* (1930).

necessity of repressing our urges to kill and rape, which leaves us psychologically discontented. One route out of those discontents is to remove civilisation altogether. In *Women in Love* (1920) by D. H. Lawrence, lovers Birkin and Ursula discuss the apocalypse while out for a stroll:

'I abhor humanity, I wish it was swept away. It could go, and there would be no *absolute* loss, if every human being perished tomorrow. The reality would be untouched. Nay, it would be better' . . .

'So you'd like everybody in the world destroyed?' said Ursula.

'I should indeed.'

'And the world empty of people?'

'Yes truly. You yourself, don't you find it a beautiful clean thought, a world empty of people, just uninterrupted grass, and a hare sitting up?'

The pleasant sincerity of his voice made Ursula pause to consider her own proposition. And really it *was* attractive: a clean, lovely, humanless world. It was the *really* desirable. Her heart hesitated, and exulted.*

* D. H. Lawrence, *Women in Love* (Thomas Seltzer, 1920).

This vision of the death of everybody may be beautiful to Birkin, but it's only beautiful if, in some phantasmic way, we are there to observe it, if our consciousness escapes the collective extinction event to wander through the new pristineness.

There's something interesting going on with this. When we fantasise about the end of the world – as we have been doing since St John's Revelation – we feel simultaneously guilty (we're projecting the deaths of billions of people, after all) and liberated: freed from everybody else, from the myriad forces and obstacles that prevent us from *being* free. This, I suspect, is what makes the zombie apocalypses we looked at in the last chapter so grisly. In such tales the world has ended, but instead of the one-dimensional harmony of last-man solitude, the landscape is filled with people who have lost the positive potential of interpersonal interaction but retain the abilities to obstruct, threaten and overwhelm.

In comparison, Mary Shelley's *Last Man* is striding out into a world picked clean, inheriting an arena of tainted freedom – tainted because it is absolute and purchased with death – but freedom nonetheless, the ultimate perfection of privacy. This is about apocalypse as escape from the other.

Shelley's contemporary, Byron, was particularly concerned with this notion and sought to preserve a sanctum of private individuality from the crush of everything else. 'I only go out,' he wrote in his journal in 1813, 'to get me a fresh appetite for being alone.' It was after he left England in 1816 that he began to realise that the very idea of privacy was under threat, or even that it might be, to use his preferred word, cant. What one critic calls his 'pathological desire for privacy' was his growing acknowledgement that there may be no such thing.

This, perhaps, is the paradoxical force of the 'last man' trope: the strange notion that the only way to safeguard our privacy absolutely would be to eliminate everyone else. After all, hell is other people, as the phrase goes, and the appeal of this particular apocalyptic dream is not only its lonely harmony, but its tacit validation of the notion that such a harmony is worth the price of everybody else in the universe dying.

Of course, this leaves the dangerous supplement of you, still lingering on after the disease has caused a collective extinction. And that brings us back to reality. To the way coronavirus has confronted Shelley's last-man fantasy of perfect mobility with a reality of lockdown and house arrest. It seems facile to note that the fantasy of plague-apocalypse is different to the reality, but the situation is more extreme than that – in fact, the fantasy and the reality are diametrically opposed to one another.

However, this is all wrong. Ultimately, humans are social creatures; the majority of us rely on the connections and interactions we have with each other – don't we? Society is built on them. Disease does not just threaten death, whether individually or on a mass scale, but devastation to the way we live our lives through, and with, one another.

Helen Marshall's fantasy novel *The Migration* (2019) is a beautiful meditation on the horrors and strange potentials of disease in such terms. One character notes:

> Disease shaped our development, and on a biological rather than a superficial level. Our genome is riddled with the debris of ancient viruses, invaders, colonizers who inserted their genes into our own. They changed us, and we changed them in return . . . Think about this: it was only when people began to gather in large communities, during the Neolithic period, that the opportunities for disease to spread increased dramatically.*

---

* Helen Marshall, *The Migration* (Random House, 2019), pp. 44–45.

The core truth of disease is that it correlates with physical intimacy. If we are physically intimate with somebody who is ill, we are liable to get ill ourselves. If we separate from us those who are ill – from large-scale projects like leper colonies down to simple precautions, such as keeping a sick child at home rather than sending them into school – we contain the spread of contagion. The coronavirus lockdown in 2020 emphasised this banal but powerful truth, but it also brought home its overwhelming correlative: just as disease involves intimacy, so intimacy actualises disease. We might be scared of being intimate with other people but more often we *desire* such intimacy – it's reassuring, pleasurable and exciting.

There is an intuitive linking of plague and sex.* Think of John Donne's erotic poem 'The Flea', in which the bloodsucking insect (a vector in the spread of bubonic and septicemic plague) becomes associated with sexual intimacy:

* The English word 'plague' comes from the Latin *plāga*, which means *wound* or *cut*, and which in Roman times had a rude slang meaning relating to female sexual organs. The English *cut*, via its older variant *cunt*, has the same double meaning.

Mark but this flea, and mark in this,
How little that which thou deniest me is;
It sucked me first, and now sucks thee,
And in this flea our two bloods mingled be;
Thou know'st that this cannot be said
A sin, nor shame, nor loss of maidenhead,
　　Yet this enjoys before it woo,
　　And pampered swells with one blood made of two,
　　And this, alas, is more than we would do.

Before the 2020 pandemic, the greatest plague panic of recent times was AIDS, a debilitating and potentially fatal autoimmune disease passed from person to person by – among other mechanisms – unprotected sexual intercourse. We are at our most intimate during sex, which both provides our most intense pleasure and is how we bring new life into the world. For sex to become the potential vector not merely of non-fatal sexually transmitted disease but also of a new deadly contaminant that turns sex into death is a peculiarly culturally potent eventuality. Sex makes us, and if we believe that it can literally unmake us, it's not surprising that we will become fascinated and repelled by it.

Through the 1980s and 1990s, AIDS provided the focus for anxious and hysterical pseudo-moralistic commentary about sex. In March 1983, reviewing a TV documentary about the new phenomenon of what was then called 'full-blown AIDS' for the *Observer*, Martin Amis wrote:

> It seems to be promiscuity itself that is the cause. After a few hundred 'tricks' or sexual contacts, the body just doesn't want to know any more, and nature proceeds to peel you wide open. The truth, when we find it, may turn out to be less 'moral', less totalitarian. Meanwhile, however, that is what it looks like.

The truth turned out to be nothing whatsoever like this panicky overreaction – you are, of course, just as likely to get HIV from unprotected sex on your first as your thousandth encounter. Health professionals were proportionate in their response to this dangerous and distressing but, ultimately, not world-ending disease; popular culture was not so measured. AIDS captured exactly the sweet spot where desire and disgust fold into one another, where sex and death become the same thing.

AIDS, like any disease, is an individual experience, but AIDS as a cultural phenomenon was seen by many as a *global* judgement. It marked what I regard as the integral logic of apocalypse: the local and particular projected upon the total; our individual mortality iterated as the death of everybody and everything. In the words of Susan Sontag, 'the AIDS crisis is evidence of a world in which nothing important is regional, local, limited; in which everything that can circulate does, and every problem is, or is destined to become, worldwide'.*

HIV/AIDS is still a threat, although it is a less present global danger than used to be the case. Although there is still no cure, nowadays antiviral drugs and other therapies render it a chronic rather than a fatal infection. In 2004, the disease's peak year, the fatality rate for sufferers was 50 per cent higher, globally, than in 2020, and that number continues to fall.

Nevertheless, AIDS continues to affect our collective imagination in a way that other plagues do not, including those that were by any objective metric much more destructive. The Spanish flu outbreak of 1918–20 killed five times as many people as AIDS has over fifty years, but after it happened it was basically forgotten – at least, until the coronavirus outbreak of 2020, which reminded us all of it once again. The Spanish flu killed

---

* Susan Sontag, *AIDS and Its Metaphors* (Farrar, Straus and Giroux, 1989), p. 180.

off several per cent of the entire global population, more than died in the century's two world wars, and the authorities flailed in response. Some did what they could: San Francisco, for instance, brought in draconian public health laws, restricting shaking hands and mandating face masks for citizens in public places. John Ryle notes that because of such measures 'there were only a few thousand deaths in San Francisco during the first year of the pandemic', but adds that 'elsewhere, including Europe, the toll was much higher. In Alaska and Central Africa and Oceania entire communities were wiped out.' He goes on:

> In statistical terms it was the greatest natural disaster since the Black Death, yet the Great Influenza Epidemic (or Pandemic) of 1918–19 has vanished from public consciousness. Unlike the war that immediately preceded it, the flu has left scarcely a trace in modern literature; historical accounts of it are sparse. One of its few chroniclers claimed that 'the Spanish Lady inspired no songs, no legends, no work of art'.*

* John Ryle, 'Zero Grazing', *London Review of Books*, 5 November 1992, p. 13.

Why didn't the Spanish flu leave a greater cultural footprint? Where are all the great novels and films about that appalling global catastrophe? The answer may have to do with timing. The Great War had facilitated the spread of the disease, since it involved millions of people being moved around the globe, as troops or refugees. But the Great War also dominated the post-war imagination in a way that the Great Flu did not. War gave us heroes and antagonists, enemies with faces against which we could pit ourselves; flu gave us none of those things.

This collective amnesia ended in 2020 with the arrival of a new virus, Covid-19. In the global lockdown that followed, the long history of flu and flu-like viruses came crashing back into our lives, and the entire planet revised their knowledge of epidemiology. Our lives were entirely changed by the trauma of loved ones getting sick and dying, but also by the disruption of lockdown, which overnight completely transformed our societies.

It's too early to say how coronavirus will factor into our ongoing general fascination with the end of the world. But it illustrates a core truth about human beings: we *are* our interactions with others – our friendships and sex lives, our workplace interactions and social media, our family and friends and the kindnesses we show strangers. Those who live as hermits, sealed away from human interaction, are the exceptions to the norm. Our existence is woven from a great many human intimacies – we require them to acquire empathy and social skills, to love and even to speak. That network of various intimacies defines us, but it is also what disease *is*: not merely the potential infections of particular germs or viruses, but the actualisation of contagion in the world.

And this is the crucial thing. Our understanding of disease, and our improved medical science, make the gloomier prognostications of science fiction doomsayers less and less likely. No plague will kill 4,999 out of every 5,000 humans – as we've seen, even if the numbers are high, in terms of percentage of population it's likely to be very low. It feels like being a hostage to fortune, writing as I am in the middle of the Covid-19 lockdown, but it is true nonetheless: disease by itself won't bring about the end of the world. But the world that emerges, post lockdown, will surely look different, and perhaps very different, to the one we knew before. We will learn new modes of remote social interaction, distanced and masked, separated into more atomised little units. Plague may not prove the end of the world – but it might be the end of the world as we know it.

4

THE AGE OF THE MACHINE: TECHNOLOGY UNLEASHED

In 1958 American author Peter George wrote a best-selling novel called *Red Alert*, concerning a mentally unbalanced and paranoid US general called Quinten who launches a nuclear attack on the USSR. Both American and Soviet governments struggle to call off the attack, but then Quinten, the only man who knows the recall codes, kills himself. Eventually all but one of the bombers are recalled, but the destruction of a Soviet city is set to provoke global war. In a desperate attempt to avert such disaster, the US president offers the Soviet premier the opportunity to destroy Atlantic City, as compensation.

It is hardly surprising following the dropping of atomic bombs, and the development of the Cold War with its arms race between the USA and USSR, that the fear of nuclear apocalypse was weighing on people's minds. It illustrates the clear possibility that humans may well be the cause of our own demise; that we can't be trusted not to use technology, however destructive it might be.

The success of *Red Alert* led to various imitators, including one by Eugene Burdick and Harvey Wheeler called *Fail-Safe* (1962), in which a nuclear attack is launched on the Soviet Union when a civilian airliner is misidentified as an enemy plane. The US bombers cannot be recalled and although most are shot down one gets through and is set to destroy Moscow. The US president phones the Russians and promises to destroy New York City with US weapons to balance out the destruction and avert total war.

Both books also inspired film deals: Stanley Kubrick's *Dr. Strangelove or: How I Learned to Stop Worrying and Love the Bomb*, based on *Red Alert*, and *Fail Safe*, directed by Sidney Lumet. *Strangelove* is now an acknowledged classic, while *Fail Safe* is forgotten. This may have something to do with the fact that, due to various reasons, Strangelove came out in January 1964 to widespread acclaim, while *Fail Safe* came out eight months later to a lukewarm reception, having missed the hype. But it might also be because it is po-faced and period-specific, while in *Strangelove* the use of comedy in portraying the world's end keeps the material fresh, even though the film's details are just as period-specific as *Fail Safe*.

In Kubrick's rewrite of the *Red Alert* storyline, the insane Brigadier General Jack D. Ripper rants about how communists are polluting his 'precious bodily fluids' as justification for his nuclear attack. Peter Sellers plays three roles: the US president Merkin Muffley, an upper-class British air force officer, Group Captain Lionel Mandrake, who remains agonisingly polite despite being kidnapped at gunpoint by Ripper, and Dr Strangelove himself. The latter is a creepy ex-Nazi scientist, modelled in part on the real-life rocket scientist Wernher von Braun. The action is divided between the British airbase from which the attack has been launched and which the US are attempting to recapture, and the US war room, from where the president and his advisors are attempting to stave off disaster.

Strangelove, confined to a wheelchair, has what appears to be an artificial hand that is prone to making inappropriate Nazi salutes* and even attempts to throttle its owner. He believes that nuclear war might be winnable, with senior US figures hiding in bunkers until the radioactivity diminishes. In order to repopulate the human race, says Strangelove, these survivors will 'regrettably' have to abandon 'the so-called monogamous sexual relationship'. It will be ten women for every man, he insists: 'a sacrifice required for the future of the human race'.

The darkly hilarious thrust of Kubrick's satire is that the people attracted to attempt the prevention of the apocalypse are precisely the kind of people who are aroused by its prospect. Sellers was contracted to play a fourth role, the pilot of the one B-52 that is not recalled when the attack is finally called off (on account of its radio being broken), and which drops its bomb. However, he was unable to master the Texas accent required for the role, and the part was played by US actor Slim Pickens instead – Pickens rides his bomb to its target like a rodeo horse, whooping with delight. The

---

* Not that I'm suggesting there are such things as *appropriate* Nazi salutes.

film ends with shots of mushroom clouds sprouting all around the world, as Vera Lynn sings 'We'll Meet Again'.

The humour certainly works; jokes, after all, emphasise the things that people try to hide away, pointing out the absurdities of our habits and hypocrisies and upending our expectations. And what could be more absurd than nuclear apocalypse; humans unable to stop themselves from bringing about the end of the world? We have good reason to fear what is – perhaps – our natural inclination towards destruction.

Assuming we don't intentionally use our own technology to destroy ourselves, the machines may come after us on their own. Science fiction is brimming with tales of caution around losing control of our creations, of artificial intelligence surpassing human intelligence and deciding we are superfluous. This is nothing new: right back at the beginning of science fiction, Shelley's *Frankenstein* is a tale of a man losing control of his creation, with terrible consequences. But in an age of constant technological advances and increasingly sophisticated AI, combined with our reliance on technology and machines for the way we live our lives, these stories express our fears that in our arrogant quest for advancement we may be the architects of our own destruction.

Take *The Terminator* (directed by James Cameron in 1984), which styles the end of the world as a direct result of human hubris. Humanity has constructed 'Skynet', an adaptive and intelligent worldwide neural network that resolves to eliminate all life on earth. Scenes in the movie alternate between a future of colossal destruction, in which gigantic death machines roll across landscapes littered with human skulls beneath a dark and foreboding sky, and present-day scenes, before the disaster. The reason for this is that Skynet has invented time travel in order to eliminate military threats before they are even born by killing their parents.

Terminators are human-scale killer robots, so called because their purpose is to terminate human life. Arnold Schwarzenegger's muscular non-acting adds a deliciously charmless implacability to their pursuit of our ultimate terminus. These killing machines must, according to the logic of the franchise's world-building, be 'coated' with human skin in order to travel back in time and to infiltrate our secret hideouts – although the story suggests that future humans all keep dogs, since they can 'smell' something is not right about these killer robots, so you'd think their disguise is more or less useless. But the 'real' reason why Terminators look like us is to reinforce the fact that we are the cause of our own downfall. During the course of the film their flesh tends to be ripped away to reveal the grinning metallic head of death beneath.

Of course humanity never does come to an end, thanks to a series of increasingly disappointing sequels: *Terminator 2: Judgment Day* (1991) was followed by *Terminator 3: Rise of the Machines* (2003), which in turn spawned *Terminator Salvation* (2009), *Terminator Genisys* (2015) and *Terminator: Dark Fate* (2019). Then there was the television show *Terminator: The Sarah Connor Chronicles*, the many spin-off video games, from *T2: Arcade Rampage, RoboCop Versus The Terminator* and *Terminator: Dawn of Fate* through to guest spots in *Tom Clancy's Ghost Recon* and *Mortal Kombat 11*, as well as myriad comics and novelisations. Time travel enables both good and bad guys to come back and overturn what their antagonists have done, providing an endless number of rebootable narrative possibilities. Goodies come back in time and undo the end of the world, while baddies come back in time and reset the end of the world. In the first and second movies, the end of the world is narrowly averted; in the third the *stopping* of the end of the world is narrowly averted, so the world ends again.

Science fiction fandom has a term for these deter-mined, single-minded killers: *berserkers*. This word was appropriated from Viking tradition (it refers to a war-rior who gets so carried away in battle that he fights in a terrifying frenzy – devastatingly and with no thought of injury) by the American science fiction author Fred Saberhagen in 1963. Saberhagen's berserkers are machine intelligences that are implacably life-hating and take the form of gigantic spacecraft that fly around the galaxy, compelled by their programming to seek out all life and destroy it. The berserkers were, we learn, created as an ultimate war machine by a now-extinct organic life form, the 'Builders', to help them win an interstellar war against their enemies, the 'Red Race'. For reasons that are not explained, these machines not only destroyed the Red Race but turned on their crea-tors and eliminated them too.

Saberhagen published dozens of 'berserker' short stories in the science fiction magazines of the 1960s and 1970s, later assembling them into no less than sixteen novel-length publications. But although the original stories are little read today, a great many later science fiction books and films have been influenced by the idea. Gregory Benford wrote a whole string of 'Galactic Center' novels in which humanity is forced to flee across the galaxy, pursued by implacable machine intelligences set on annihilating them. The British science fiction writer Alastair Reynolds' 'Inhibitors' sequence (the first in the series was *Revelation Space* in 2000) embroiders a similar story. The TV show *Battlestar Galactica*, commissioned in 1978 to cash in on the success of *Star Wars*, imagines a life-hating robot species called the Cylons, who persecute the last human remnants in space, having already ended their world; the flashier remake of this series (2003–9) explores the motivations of these machine intelligences in greater detail, without ever making any more sense of them.

Iterations of a similar end-of-the-world idea also occur in video games and films. The popular game *Mass Effect* (2007) is an expansive space opera in which organic life forms come under periodic attack from a life-hating alien machine species called the 'Reapers' – giant sentient and synthetic-technological starships.

As machines and technology become an increasingly fundamental part of our lives, so the tales of their uprising intensify. The most successful and resonant of all the recent stories of technological apocalypse is the Matrix trilogy. Directed by the Wachowski sisters, these films tie together several themes as well as technology: it is also religious apocalypse – the story of a saviour figure gifted with miraculous power who has come to save the world. And it is a kind of zombie, or 'techno-zombie', story, as 'Smith', the malign computer intelligence, infects increasing numbers of people, turning the global population into an army of belligerents, all focused on one destructive aim. To me it presents a fascinating portrayal of disease.

Like the best science fiction, *The Matrix* is more effective as a metaphor than as a piece of internally consistent world-building. The trilogy's premise is that human beings have been enslaved by machine intelligences in a post-apocalyptic future: our bodies are being held in individual pods and used as batteries to run the machine world. To distract us from our confinement, our minds are plugged into a collective virtual reality – the Matrix. This makes no sense on its own terms, but to pick holes in the conceit is, of course, to miss the point. These movies express a metaphorical truth about modern humanity's dependence on computers and our shift to a virtual simulacrum of life. And, as metaphor, they are as eloquent as they are cool.

The first film in the trilogy, *The Matrix*, is a classic of its genre. The movie's core conceit and many of its specific details have acquired widespread cultural currency, although its sequel, *The Matrix Reloaded* (2003), is regarded as a disappointing anticlimax, and there's even less love around for the final instalment in the trilogy, *The Matrix Revolutions* (2003). Much of this movie is narratively incoherent, but its ending finds a compromise between man and machine. After a lengthy battle with the machines' army, sent to destroy them, the humans realise they cannot win this war; Neo goes back into the Matrix to negotiate a truce with the ruling machine intelligences.

The idea of the existence of life forms more intelligent than our own clearly troubles us. If it's not our own AI coming to take us down, it's aliens. There was a time when space aliens tended to be morally as well as technologically superior to humanity. The gigantic and wise alien visitor from the star Sirius in Voltaire's *Micromégas* (1752) looks down with serene disapproval on an earth wracked by war and injustice. In many cases, nineteenth-century space aliens inhabit a purely spiritual realm, as in Marie Corelli's hugely-successful-but-now-forgotten *A Romance of Two Worlds* (1886), in which human suffering is revealed as a function of our earthboundness, and the interstellar spaces through which the novel's protagonist travels are suffused with spiritual wonder (C. S. Lewis reused the idea for his 'Space' trilogy of science fiction novels, 1938–45).

However, most science fiction now focuses on aliens as great invaders, come to end our world, and although the likelihood of such apocalypse is miniscule, this fantasy plays a large role in science fiction and popular culture.

Why the change? It seems likely that the shift between the 1750s and the 1890s was caused by the massive expansion of Western imperialism. The early eighteenth century was hardly a time of innocence in terms of the European exploitation of the rest of the world, but by the end of the nineteenth century imperialism was being pursued on a scale and with an inhumanity unprecedented in human history. It was also becoming as unignorable at 'home' as it was in those countries that were on the receiving end of imperial aggression, and fed into rising concerns over what would happen as these competing empires increasingly came into conflict with each other.

George Tomkyns Chesney's *The Battle of Dorking* (1871), a short novel about an imagined future German invasion of Britain, sparked a trend for 'invasion stories'. It is badly written, hectoring and crass, but it touched a chord of anxiety in the British public: *Blackwood's Magazine*, where the story was first published, reprinted the issue six times to meet demand, and produced as a separate volume it sold 110,000 copies in two months. Scores of similar tales appeared over the following decades, imagining future invasions by Europeans, Chinese, Americans and other peoples.

It was a particular stroke of genius by H. G. Wells to replace human adversaries with alien ones in his 1898 novel *The War of the Worlds*, not least because it so effectively changes the threat level from a local to a global one. He was imagining what it might be like to find oneself on the receiving end of this mode of apocalyptic alien expansionism. It is Wells who deserves the credit for establishing the portrayal of aliens from outer space as malign, predatory monsters bent on dominating or destroying the globe.

In *The War of the Worlds*, terrifying bear-sized, octopus-like tentacular Martian invaders crash to earth in gigantic metallic cylinders, emerging from their landing craft to pilot towering mechanical tripods that devastate south-east England. After several months of wreaking death and destruction, they succumb to mundane germs against which they have no natural defence. But you already know the story. *The War of the Worlds* is Wells's most famous novel, and has had a greater influence on the development of twentieth-century science fiction than any other (except *Frankenstein*, perhaps).

Wells's aliens are material rather than spiritual beings, more highly evolved and much more technologically adept, but uninterested in human moral orientations. They refract the idea of British imperial expansion back upon the British, bringing destruction, exploitation and death to London. As the novel goes on, we learn that 'more highly evolved' means that they have dispensed with a stomach and digestive system altogether and instead feed like vampires, taking the blood directly from other animals. They come to Earth to eat us.

Had the invaders not died of disease, it would have been a global disaster, with the subjugation of our species and the end of civilisation as we know it. But we might speculate that it would not have led to the destruction of all life on earth, as they needed to keep us around to feed on.

Nonetheless, many modern science fiction writers have explored a more extreme version of Wells's alien invasion. A great many stories and films have been written and made in which alien invaders even more malignly destructive than Wells's Martians attempt to destroy human life – perhaps most famously in Roland Emmerich's loose adaptation of Wells's novel, *Independence Day*, the highest-grossing film of 1996.

Wells's invaders are motivated by the desiccation of their home world and a desire to find a new place to live, but the ruthless alien invaders in Emmerich's movie are more like locusts, their whole civilisation predicated on the model of travelling from one planet to the next, stripping each in turn of their natural resources before moving on.

The Chinese science fiction writer Liu Cixin explores a central mystery in his novel *The Three-Body Problem*:* what does a popular immersive virtual-reality game have to do with the suicide of prominent Earth scientists? The answer is that a superior alien species known as the Trisolarans, living in a solar system many light years away, are planning an invasion that will wipe out humanity. It will take 400 years for the Trisolaran fleet to reach us, but they have already made their presence felt. Using a technology based on 'sophons', particles that transmit back everything they observe, they have been monitoring humanity and can communicate with us if they wish. This technology is so sophisticated that nothing can be hidden from the Trisolarans: they have access to all computer databases

---

* Published in 2008 in China. He was the first Chinese winner of the Hugo Award for the English translation.

and human communication. The only thing to which their surveillance does not have access is the inside of human minds.

Volume two of Liu's trilogy, *The Dark Forest* (2008), continues the story. The question is: how to defeat an all-powerful enemy you know is coming, when your every countermeasure will be observed by them? Earth comes up with an unusual plan: four individuals are carefully selected – a head of state, a scientist, a general and the story's main character, a sociologist called Luo Ji. These designated 'Wallfacers' are asked to devise a plan to save humanity, each of them working separately from the others and with all of earth's resources at their disposal. No matter how bizarre or random their requests, they must be honoured; and if they appear to be acting for arbitrary, or insane, or inane reasons – well, such randomness can only help to baffle Trisolaran surveillance. When Luo Ji, a lazy, underachieving academic, is selected for this prestigious role, he can hardly believe it, and when he tries to turn the invitation down the world assumes that he is trying to throw the Trisolarans off the scent. So he decides to accept, and to use his new power to indulge his innate hedonism. He moves into a luxurious mountain palace and orders all sorts of indulgences brought to him, including his dream girl – a fantasy of perfect femininity from his youth.

Liu Cixin dramatises his impending world's-end with aplomb. The world is divided between those who think the Trisolarans must be defeated at all costs and those who argue that Earth should build spaceships to evacuate as many citizens as possible before they arrive. In the end, the mood of the world shifts towards confrontation.

By the time the Trisolarans arrive, Earth has built a fleet of powerful space battleships to rebut the invasion and it seems the Wallfacers' plans will not be needed. However, the aliens are so technologically advanced that they make short shrift of our defences. A character called Ye Wenjie explains to Luo Ji – the only Wallfacer still active – the true nature of the cosmos:

> The universe is a dark forest. Every civilization is an armed hunter stalking through the trees like a ghost, gently pushing aside branches that block the path and trying to tread without sound . . . The hunter has to be careful, because everywhere in the forest are stealthy hunters like him. If he finds other life – another hunter, an angel or a demon, a delicate infant . . . there's only one thing he can do:

open fire and eliminate them. In this forest, hell
is other people. An eternal threat that any life that
exposes its own existence will be swiftly wiped out.*

The final volume in the trilogy, *Death's End* (2010),
concludes the story: Luo Ji uses the threat of mutually
assured destruction to force the Trisolarans into a truce:
if they attack Earth, he will broadcast their existence
throughout the universe, and more terrifying species
will come hunting for them both. An uneasy peace
ensues, although it does not last. The Trisolaran system
is annihilated by forces even more powerful than them
and they flee, believing that Earth will be next. The story
doesn't quite end there, but that's where we'll leave it
for the moment.

If we're terrified that technology will destroy us –
whether by our own hand or someone else's – we seem
to be equally afraid that it can't save us. In another
space-related end-of-the-world scenario, the thing that
smashes the planet to pieces is not sentient, and is
guided not by hostility but by chance. From planets to
asteroids, the vast reaches of space contain a multitude

---

*   Liu Cixin, *The Dark Forest* (Head of Zeus, 2015), p. 484.

of objects that could spell our end – and in these stories, technology is now our only hope.

The key modern version of this kind of world's end is the movie *When Worlds Collide* (directed by Rudolph Maté in 1951), the success of which kick-started the 1950s boom in science fiction filmmaking. Based on two 1930s science fiction novels by Philip Wylie and Edwin Balmer (*When Worlds Collide* and its sequel, *After Worlds Collide*), Maté's movie tells the story of an astronomer called Emery Bronson who detects a rogue star called Bellus. He deduces that Bellus will crash into Earth, causing the end of the world. When Bronson presents his findings to the United Nations he is mocked, but a group of prescient millionaires finance the construction of a new spaceship called 'Noah's Ark' and plan to fly on to the star's lone planet, Zyra, which they determine is habitable. In the end, the spaceship launches and takes forty humans to a new life on Zyra.

The movie still carries a punch, and it has also spawned imitators. In *The Day the Earth Caught Fire* (1961), Soviet and US nuclear tests accidentally knock the Earth closer to the Sun, with devastating results. In *Meteor* (1979), a giant meteor is detected on a world-ending collision course with Earth, before catastrophe is eventually averted. In 1998, two movies – *Armageddon* and *Deep Impact* – were released in which brave men fly up on space shuttles to avert an impending world-ending meteor strike with nuclear bombs. Lars von Trier's arthouse movie *Melancholia* (2011) is lower-key: a rogue planet is on a collision course with the world, but this one is a disaster that cannot be averted. The movie follows the lives of two sisters, played by Kirsten Dunst and Charlotte Gainsbourg, until the blue planet collides with the world and everything is brought to a final end. That this planet 'Melancholia' is an obvious metaphor for suicidal depression (from which Kirsten Dunst's character suffers) does not rob the movie of its force, or the dark beauty of its final shots.

There is a grim but satisfying physicality in imagining the world being smacked, as if by an enormous cosmic hammer. Although we find it hard to picture the ongoing slowly increasing toxicity of our natural environment, we *can* picture a fist punching through a plank of wood laid out over two breeze blocks. It is immediate and speaks to our direct experience: war in the twentieth century was dominated by aerial bombing, and as the catastrophic damage and death it caused became a feature of wartime experience, the temptation to extrapolate this and imagine a cosmic bomb dropped onto Earth from space led to these particular apocalyptic movies.

Nor is this mere paranoia – it is prudent to watch the skies for asteroids, because a large enough celestial object colliding with our world would end it, in a literal sense. And there are good reasons to fear such a catastrophe. After all, it has happened before. In fact, the Earth has been the site of *five* major asteroid-prompted extinctions, as well as a dozen lesser ones. The first such catastrophe happened some 450 million years ago, during the late Ordovician Period. Around 250 million years ago, during the Permian-Triassic Period, a global disaster destroyed 90 per cent of all marine life, and 65 million years ago an asteroid the size of Edinburgh hurtled down onto the Yucatán Peninsula, landing with a force equivalent to 100 million hydrogen bombs. The professor of biology and earth sciences Peter Ward describes 'life's worst day on Earth' as follows:

The world's global forest burned to the ground, absolute darkness from dust clouds encircled the earth for six months, acid rain burned the shells off of calcareous plankton, and a tsunami picked up all of the dinosaurs on the vast, Cretaceous coastal plains, drowned them, and then hurled their carcasses against whatever high elevations finally subsided the monster waves.*

This, as Ward notes, was 'death writ large', and the fact that it has happened multiple times before makes it likely to happen again. According to the B612 Foundation (a California-based non-profit that studies near-Earth objects for potential impact and lobbies for the development of better defences against them), the probability that an asteroid as large as the one that destroyed the Tunguska River area in Russia in 1908 will strike us during the twenty-first century is 30 per cent. The earth is much more widely and densely populated than in previous eras, so the risk of large casualties is correspondingly higher. The possibility of a planet-ending asteroid strike is not trivial.† And should one appear in the sights of a telescope one day, what will we do about it? Can science and technology save us? Or must we resign ourselves to our final fate?

---

* Peter Ward, 'Nautilus and Me', Nautilus, 29 April 2013: http://nautil.us/issue/0/the-story-of-nautilus/ingenious-nautilus-and-me

† The organisation's website makes for absorbing, if often terrifying, reading: https://b612foundation.org/

We have had to come to terms with the reality of our place in the universe – not at its centre, the most important place to be, but a miniscule speck hanging precariously in an unimaginably vast, unforgiving, uncaring void. We need our technology to reassure us that we can protect ourselves against it. We need it to enable our explorations of space, to reassert our importance, to prove our superior intelligence – especially should an alien neighbour show up. And yet, fully aware of the weaknesses of our own nature, we also still fear technology, what it might do to us, and what we might do with it to ourselves.

5

HEAT DEATHS AND ETERNAL RETURNS: THE END OF THE UNIVERSE

In 1895 H. G. Wells wrote of a 'time traveller' (the novel does not disclose his name) who has created a machine that can transport him backwards or forwards in time. He opts for the latter, zooms to the year 802,701 and discovers that humanity has evolved, or rather 'devolved', into two separate species: the beautiful but stupid Eloi, who live idly and hedonistically above ground, and the technologically advanced but hideously ugly Morlocks, who live below ground and come out at night to feast on the Eloi.

That's the most famous part of *The Time Machine*, but after this episode the traveller travels even further into the future and sees further 'devolution', with mankind becoming rabbit-like creatures and then crab-like monsters, scuttling around under a dying sun. The final portion of the story takes us from the year 802,701 to the year 802,701,600,509,408,307,206,105,004,* the final epoch of the world, where all life has been distilled into a strange, half-seen, uncanny globular creature:

> The darkness grew apace; a cold wind began to blow in freshening gusts from the east, and the showering white flakes in the air increased in number. From the edge of the sea came a ripple and whisper. Beyond these lifeless sounds the world was silent. Silent? It would be hard to convey the stillness of it. All the sounds of man, the bleating of sheep, the cries of birds, the hum of insects, the stir that makes the background of our lives – all that was

---

* Actually Wells doesn't specify the year in which his final chapters are set, but this seems to me as good a guess as any.

over. As the darkness thickened, the eddying flakes grew more abundant, dancing before my eyes; and the cold of the air more intense [. . .] In another moment the pale stars alone were visible. All else was rayless obscurity. The sky was absolutely black.

A horror of this great darkness came on me. The cold, that smote to my marrow, and the pain I felt in breathing, overcame me. I shivered, and a deadly nausea seized me [. . .] I felt I was fainting. But a terrible dread of lying helpless in that remote and awful twilight sustained me while I clambered upon the saddle.

This dark conclusion is indicative of something profound. In this story Wells creates a machine that promises an ultimate freedom, an escape from the 'now', with the whole of our past and future available to explore. It is the fantasy of escaping mortality, for what is death but the formal structure of the inevitability of our various individual timelines? Wells's brilliance was to grasp that the escape route from death is not actually an escape but rather leads back to death; the death of the individual becomes the death of the species. There's a reason why Wells's terminal beach has proved so iconic for science fiction writers

– J. G. Ballard even wrote a short story called 'The Terminal Beach'.

I would argue that *The Time Machine* is one of the most influential works of science fiction ever written, but it is also a masterpiece of a particular genre of end-of-the-world fiction – the dying earth. It came at a time when advances were being made towards understanding the nature of the universe, allowing scientists to finally develop more accurate theories regarding the workings and ultimate fate of our Sun – the very thing that brings light and life to our planet.

The Sun is a fire, so there will logically come a time when it burns itself out. That's not a comforting thought: without a sun, the world will grow cold and dark and we will all die. People have been speculating about such end times for centuries. In the seventeenth century, the English naturalist and scientist John Ray argued that the sunspots, or 'maculae', we can see on the face of the Sun were symptoms that it was starting to die. His *Miscellaneous Discourses Concerning the Dissolution and Changes of the World* (1692) includes this prophesy:

After some vast Periods of Time, the Sun may be so inextricably enveloped by the *Maculae*, that he

may quite lose his Light; and then you may easily guess what would become of the Inhabitants of
the Earth.*

In the nineteenth century, scientists were particularly
worried about the Sun going out. New discoveries about
the actual age of the Earth combined with all the obser-
vations they had made told them the Sun should have
burnt through its fuel long ago. In 1871, the British
scientist William Mattieu Williams noted that even
though the Sun's 'stupendous ocean of explosive gases'
constituted 'an enormous stock of fuel', it should have
been used up over the millions of years the Earth had
existed. Long before the present, he calculated, there
should have been 'a gradual diminution of the amount
of solar radiation, and a slow and perpetually retarding
progress towards solar extinction'.

The solution to this conundrum was not discovered until 1904, when the physicist Ernest Rutherford
speculated that radioactive decay at the core of the
Sun might provide it with its energy. Albert Einstein's
work provided the frame by which Rutherford's insight
could be theorised, and in 1920 Sir Arthur Eddington

* John Ray, *Three Physico-Theological Discourses* (1715), p. 315.

argued that the extreme pressures and temperatures at the Sun's heart cause a nuclear fusion reaction, squeezing hydrogen atoms together with such force that they merge into helium nuclei, releasing considerable quantities of energy as a result. This is still our best understanding of why the Sun burns; nobody has travelled to the Sun to check, but we're pretty sure.

But although this explains why the Sun has burnt for as long as it has, it only kicks the can down the road. For though the Sun's fuel will last for billions of years, our star *will* eventually burn through all its fuel. And when that happens, the constitution of the Sun will alter and any life forms in the vicinity will die.

When the metaphorical fuel-tank indicator needle starts wobbling near zero, four things will happen, which we might regard as four apocalyptic horsemen. First, the Sun will swell hugely, becoming a red giant (let's call this the *red horse* stage), which will gobble up the inner planets, assuming they are still in those orbits in five billion years' time.* The red phase will last

* Spoiler: they won't be. The overwhelming likelihood is that none of the planets currently orbiting the Sun will be in their present orbits by that point. The thing to keep in mind is that our Sun is sweeping in a great arc around the outer hem of our galaxy; five billion years of its future will include many close encounters with

for 100 million years or so, until the Sun shrinks to a much smaller, dimmer version of its former self (the *pale horse*), which will last as long as 500 million years before eventually the outer layers of the Sun will blast away, leaving only the brilliant white core (the *white horse*). At this point, all of the fuel has run out, it burns only because its constitutive elements are very hot; over time, perhaps trillions of years, this heat will be radiated away and the Sun will reach its final state: a lightless black dwarf (the *black horse*).

It doesn't stop there. If our Sun will die, then so too will all the stars in the universe. And while new stars are being born even as I write, it will not always be that way. Eventually all the stars will have used up their fuel, and will stop shining. Then, for unimaginable gulfs of time, the universe will be black, cold, inert, over and forever continuing to be over.

Almost all scientists agree that the universe began with the Big Bang, when a dimensionless point 'exploded', pouring out matter in all directions. This

other stars and gravitationally significant objects liable to interfere with the orbital mechanics of the solar system, even to the point of slingshotting planets out of solar orbit altogether. Then again, it's also likely the Sun will pick up new satellites in that time, so there's a reasonable chance that it will have *something* to nibble on as it swells.

universal expansion is an ongoing, measurable phenomenon. As the matter continues to expand outwards, becoming less dense, new stars will no longer form. Eventually, over quadrillions of years, each and every existing star in the universe will use up its fuel. The unimaginably vast spaces of the expanding cosmos will be diluted to a temperature only slightly above absolute zero.

The technical term for this process is 'entropy', a word with a vulgar as well as a scientific meaning. The latter dates from 1865, but the former, which is much older, is that *things run down*. From ancient times, humans have understood this basic truth about the nature of things – that order slowly becomes disorder, as youth inevitably decays into age. Build your house, fit its windows and paint its walls, by all means; you know very well that unless you keep inputting your labour, it will fall away into crumbling, peeling, weed-clogged disorder. That's the crude sense of what entropy means: disorder increases unless we put in the work to maintain order.

So this is the end that most scientists tell us is coming: a cold universe expanding lightlessly, lifelessly and forever, however hot, bright and lively things are right now. Not a very heartening prospect.

While theories over the fate of our sun developed and were widely disseminated through the eighteenth and nineteenth centuries, they took root in popular imagination, prompting some wonderfully gloomy examples of the end, perhaps most marvellously Byron's long poem 'Darkness' (1816), which begins:

I had a dream, which was not all a dream.
The bright sun was extinguish'd, and the stars
Did wander darkling in the eternal space,
Rayless, and pathless, and the icy earth
Swung blind and blackening in the moonless air;
Morn came and went – and came, and brought no day,
And men forgot their passions in the dread
Of this their desolation; and all hearts
Were chill'd into a selfish prayer for light:
And they did live by watchfires – and the thrones,
The palaces of crowned kings – the huts,
The habitations of all things which dwell,
Were burnt for beacons; cities were consum'd,
And men were gather'd round their blazing homes
To look once more into each other's face;
Happy were those who dwelt within the eye
Of the volcanos, and their mountain-torch:
A fearful hope was all the world contain'd;

Forests were set on fire – but hour by hour
They fell and faded – and the crackling trunks
Extinguish'd with a crash – and all was black.

Byron's poem ends unambiguously: it's all over, and
everybody and everything is dead. The last words of the
poem are 'Darkness had no need / Of aid from them –
She was the Universe.'

Byron, a rock-and-roll rebel centuries before the
concept was invented, is doing what any intelligent
atheist might do: he's looking into the future and seeing nothing but decay, death and extinction. Without
something supernatural outside the universe to input
newness, the cosmos will inevitably be governed by the
logic of everything running down.

The question is, why should we find this scenario
so gloomy? It's the end of course but not one that is
in any way imminent – it is trillions of years down the
line. To astrophysicists it's a mere flicker in the long
duration of our collective future, but hardly of concern
to the rest of us as individuals, or even as a species.
Mammals have an average species lifespan of about a
million years, which makes it unlikely we'll even survive to the point when the increasing brightness of our
sun makes our planet uninhabitable in about a billion

years' time. But perhaps there's something about knowing that the universe is just as doomed as we are that makes us uncomfortable.

We might be able to accept the idea of our own mortality in the knowledge that it's not the end of our collective story; humankind will carry on without us, marching towards its ultimate goal, whatever that may be. The survival of the human race is a key concern in nearly every apocalyptic scenario. But if all we're ultimately heading towards is the end of something, then what, really, is the point of it all?

Such a line of thought can inspire quite the pessimistic outlook on life. Among philosophers, whose business is understanding how things are rather than telling heartening stories about how they might be, this ultimate pessimism is fairly common. The Romanian thinker Emil Cioran looked with an unfazed eye at a cosmos ruled by entropy: 'someday the old shack we call the world will fall apart', he noted passionlessly. 'How, we don't know, and we don't really care either. Since nothing has real substance, and life is a twirl in the void, its beginning and its end are meaningless.'*

---

* Emil Cioran, *Tears and Saints*, translated by Ilinka Zarifopol-Johnston (University of Chicago Press, 1995), p. 23.

The grandfather of this sort of philosophical pessimism was Arthur Schopenhauer, a man who was so moody that his own mother wrote him a letter saying: 'You are unbearable and burdensome, and very hard to live with; all your good qualities are overshadowed by your conceit, and made useless to the world simply because you cannot restrain your propensity to pick holes in other people.' Schopenhauer saw the cosmos as a whole as vastly more miserable than it is happy, and so, on a cosmic level, his view was that not only is the non-existence of this world just as possible as its existence, but that the former is preferable to the latter. Had Schopenhauer known about modern physics' vision of the cold, inert sterility with which our universe will end, he might have regarded it positively.

But most people shy away from the idea of such a final ending. There's always a loophole to find: if our world is doomed, we'll hop over to Mars. If our sun is set to go out, by then we'll have travelled to some distant galaxy. But what Wells is really saying with his terminal beach is: eventually you run out of escape hatches. Eventually we will run out of time and space.

Are scientists sure that the universe will end this way? The short answer is that they're not, because scientists don't deal in absolute certainties. Science deals in hypotheses that are more or less widely held but never proved, because they are always open to falsification.* And science is a story, just as religion, myth and fiction also are. I don't mean to suggest that it is no better at accurately describing the universe than those other things – I consider it to be in almost every respect a more truthful account of the universe when it is buttressed with data, experimental replicability and conceptual consistency, but scientists do nonetheless tell stories. So even if most modern-day astrophysicists think heat death is where we are heading, some of them believe the end will be something else, a version of the end in which rebirth and renewal may be possible. We've seen it in religious myth already, that vision of the end of the world where, instead of slowly dying out, the world springs up again after the apocalypse, reborn anew, but how could that work?

Well, it's possible that the Big Bang will at some point go into reverse. All the matter flung out in that

---

* 'Falsification' is the philosopher Karl Popper's *de facto* definition of science. A biological scientist might advance the rule 'all swans are white'; if we spot a black swan, then we have falsified that universal. The important thing to note is that falsification is not the same thing as *an absolute refutation*. When faced with data that falsifies a theory, a scientist usually modifies it ('most swans are white').

initial detonation has mass, which entails gravity. Some scientists believe that the gravity of the trillions of star-dense galaxies will slow down the expansion, stop it and then slowly pull everything back towards itself again. This would result in a 'Big Crunch', with all the matter in the universe falling towards a central point increasingly rapidly. And maybe the energy of the entire mass of the universe collapsing in on itself would put so much pressure on its now miniscule portion of space-time that gravity would be momentarily distorted, and everything would blast outward again in a second Big Bang, a 'Big Bounce'.

The theory was more widely believed in the past than it is now. It still has some adherents in the scientific community, but according to the most up-to-date science, neither the 'Big Crunch' nor the 'Big Bounce' theories are true. We won't collapse back, and we won't bounce – we will instead wind down slowly. Entropy, rather than rebirth, wins the day.

Are we sure? The answer depends on how heavy the universe is, since gravity is the force that will draw the cosmos's matter back into a new singularity. If the mass of the whole universe is dense enough, there will be enough gravity to slow our expansion and eventually reverse it. But the most current science suggests that the mass of the universe is below that threshold, and that it will not have enough gravitational attraction to fall back in on itself.*

Nevertheless, it is the idea of escape and rebirth that science fiction tends to cleave to. 'Eucatastrophe' is a term invented by J. R. R. Tolkien to describe the sorts of stories he himself wrote, in *The Lord of the Rings* for instance. The 'eu' in 'eucatastrophe' means *good*, and Tolkien was talking about those sorts of stories in which things seem bad until they swerve towards good at the last moment. Consider those tales where events get worse and worse until we reach a point where the whole situation appears hopeless. In tragedy, that is where the story ends and we leave the theatre or close the book sadder but wiser. But the last hundred years or so have proved allergic to tragedy, and we are nowadays much more interested in eucatastrophe – in the final twist in which evil is defeated in the nick of time, when the giant asteroid plummeting towards Earth is averted at the very last moment. Eucatastrophe is when the storyteller makes a happy ending out of a

---

* Indeed, modern scientists note that the cosmic expansion actually appears to be *speeding up*. They don't know why, and explain the increase in expansion with reference to something they call 'dark energy'.

doomy situation, just as a conjurer pulls a rabbit from a top hat. We saw this with the religious and mythological apocalypses of the previous chapters. The world ends in fire or via enormous human suffering and death, and then – miraculously – a new world appears, clean and bright.

The truth is that although science fiction likes to pride itself on the 'science' part of its name, it is more informed by religious thinking than it cares to admit. The ends of the world in science fiction, after all, are generally religious apocalypses in a pseudo-scientific overcoat and hat, taking us through suffering in order to emerge somewhere new. This is a book about the representations of the end of the world, but in actual fact it is hardly ever represented.

Entropy is a real-life phenomenon, but naturally enough we tend to want to cling to our stories of more optimistic 'endings' even in the face of scientific evidence. It's striking how few writers have followed Wells and Byron down the pessimistic route of the eternal freeze, even as the scientific discoveries piled up.

A few years before Byron's 'Darkness', the scientist-poet Erasmus Darwin (grandfather of Charles Darwin) published an epic poem called *The Botanic Garden* that also turned a clear eye on the likely end of things. Its apprehension of the end of the cosmos is no jollier than Byron's:

> Flowers of the sky! ye too to age must yield,
> Frail as your silken sisters of the field!
> Star after star from heaven's high arch shall rush,
> Suns sink on suns, and systems systems crush,
> Headlong, extinct, to one dark centre fall,
> And death and night and chaos mingle all!*

However, Darwin was no Byron. He worked for the betterment of humanity and was a firm believer in God; he tempers the gloominess of this vision with some more hopeful lines:

> Till o'er the wreck, emerging from the storm,
> Immortal Nature lifts her changeful form,
> Mounts from her funeral pyre on wings of flame,
> And soars and shines, another and the same.

William Hope Hodgson's novel *The Night Land* (1912) is set after the death of the sun, but the story concerns the *survival* of humankind after that catastrophe

---

* Erasmus Darwin, *The Botanic Garden* (1791), 4.2.378–83.

– survivors have holed up inside a gigantic pyramid called 'the last redoubt', powered by residual heat from inside the earth. More usually, science fiction authors set their stories shortly *before* the death of the sun, enabling a melancholic and elegiac style of storytelling. The American author Jack Vance's short novel *The Dying Earth* (1950) initiated the vogue for this sort of storytelling, which is now known as 'dying earth fiction', but Vance's wit and ornate inventiveness are a long way from the desolation of Wells's terminal beach. Perhaps the work of 'dying earth' science fiction with the highest reputation is Gene Wolfe's four-volume 'The Book of the New Sun' (1980–83): a major work of literature in which an apprentice torturer called Severian travels through a world that is at once medieval and high-tech, and over which a dying sun is giving out its last light. Wolfe is as inventive as Vance but not so irreverent, and he tackles the end of the world with gravity and integrity. But he was also a Catholic, and rather than follow through the remorselessly entropic logic of his novels, he wrote a sequel, *The Urth of the New Sun* (1987), in which Severian rejuvenates the dying sun and renews his world.

James Blish's classic quartet of Golden Age science fiction novels, known collectively as 'Cities in Flight'

(1955–62), ends when inhabitants of spacefaring human cities discover that the collapse of the cosmos has been accelerated and a Big Crunch is imminent. Knowing that the crunch will annihilate all life in the cosmos and that a new universe will burst forth, Blish's characters contrive to find a way to pass something immaterial – love – to shape the logic of the new universe.

It's not just science fiction writers exploring the idea. The scientist Frank Tipler isn't satisfied with the idea of such evanescent 'influence' on the next iteration of the universe; he wants to keep all human life alive forever in *this* iteration. His book *The Physics of Immortality: Modern Cosmology, God and the Resurrection of the Dead* (1994) argues that such immortality is not only possible but inevitable. He calls the Big Crunch the 'Omega Point' and seeks to show that it will be a transcendent climax of cosmic information-processing. Intelligence, he argues, will use asymmetries in the shrinking to generate effectively unlimited energy, which will in turn power far-future iterations of computers that will run perfect digital copies of all the people who have ever lived in immaculate digital worlds. Time, he says, will be made to run asymptotically – that is, after the manner of a hyperbolic curve that steepens and steepens without ever quite becoming vertical – such that it *feels* infinite to these copies, who will be indistinguishable from resurrected human consciousnesses.

Though he is a respected cosmologist, Tipler was widely mocked for the earnest literalism with which he works through his heavenly vision in this book. He addresses such minutiae as 'Will my dog be resurrected along with me?' (His answer: the collective intelligence of the Omega Point will want us to be happy – if our happiness depends upon us having our dog with us, then we'll have them with us.) But it is, in many ways, as pure an iteration of religious apocalypse as anything by St John – a eucatastrophic vision of inevitable disaster averted at the last moment.

But there's a fundamental point to consider with this theory: why should this be the second Big Bang? Why should the universe we're living in at the moment be the very first? Maybe our current reality is the millionth version, and the next Big Bang will be the million-and-first. Or maybe this process of Big Bang, Big Crunch and Big Bounce has been going on forever. If you continue down this line of thought it turns out there is only one thing more depressing than the prospect of the cosmos winding down to a state of eternal cold, dark, lifeless nullity: the prospect of it *not* doing that.

Consider this: every possible combination of the universe's atoms would reoccur *an infinite number of times*. If the universe is a finite number of atoms being juggled across an infinite timescale, your exact life will be lived not once but *an infinite number of times*.

From that night you lay awake, tormented by toothache, to the birth of your children, you will live every joy, every torment, every boredom, every effort over and over, in exactly the form you have already lived it, forever. If that seems hard to believe, perhaps you don't quite grasp the magnitude of infinity.

Nietzsche was fascinated by this very idea, which he called 'the Eternal Return' (sometimes translated into English as 'the Eternal Recurrence'). He first mentions it in *The Gay Science* (1882) and explores it at greater length in his masterpiece *Thus Spoke Zarathustra* (1883–85). Some scholars will try and tell you that Nietzsche raises the issue of the Eternal Return only as a thought experiment, but don't be fooled – he literally believed in the Eternal Recurrence, and if the 'Big Bounce' theory is correct, he was quite right to. This is how he puts it:

The weightiest burden: What, if by day or night, a devil were to sneak in upon you, during your moment of loneliest loneliness and say to you:

'This life, as you now live it and have lived it, you will be compelled to live again, and again, and innumerable times again; and there will be nothing new in it, but every moment of suffering and every joy and every thought and lament and everything, whether small or great, you will return to as you live, all in the same succession and order – even *this* spider and *this* moonlight between the trees and *this* moment and your meeting here with me, myself. The eternal hourglass of existence is turned over again and again – and you with it, you mote of dust!'

Would you not throw yourself down and gnash your teeth and curse the demon who spoke to you this way? Or have you experienced that overpowering moment when you could answer him: 'You are a god, and I have never heard anything more wonderfully divine!' If this thought lodges itself inside your brain it will change you as you are – perhaps it will destroy you utterly. The question you must always ask yourself, with each and every thing you do or encounter, is this: 'do I *want* this, again, and then again, and an infinite number of times again?' Such a question would lie upon your actions as the weightiest burden imaginable. But then, perhaps, it gives you the opportunity to become the best version of yourself, to yourself, and in life to crave nothing more fervently than this ultimate eternal confirmation and seal?*

Nietzsche's point is that only the strongest soul would be able to embrace this fate – to experience with intense joy every single moment of existence, whether painful or happy, exciting or dull, even though they are doomed to repeat exactly that moment over and over again, forever. The ability to embrace this fate is the key quality of Nietzsche's celebrated 'superman' – the *Übermensch*, he thought, was destined to replace *Homo sapiens*. And the way to become an *Übermensch* is to look into your soul and know, with absolute certainty, that you truly embrace the Eternal Return.

I suspect that for many people the idea of a 'Big Bounce' appeals because it evades the horrors of the heat death story, opening a secret door through which we can escape mortality. To me its implications are, in the strict sense of the word, appalling. The thought that I would have to live my life over and over in every detail, like being trapped in an infinite loop of *Groundhog Day*,

---

* Nietzsche, *The Gay Science* (1882), p. 341.

a masterpiece of supreme existential terror,* provokes in me a profound existential revulsion. Grim though the prospect of the universal heat death is, the alternative is far worse. If those are our two options, then I know which one I'd prefer.

---

* Perhaps you think it is a charming and funny romantic comedy? You are wrong. I cannot deny that Bill Murray's deadpan performance generates many laughs from a well-written script, but if you think about it properly it is the most horrifying movie ever made. How long must he have been trapped there to learn jazz piano, ice sculpture and French? This was no two-week glitch, but one that went on for years, decades – or longer: director Harold Ramis, a Buddhist, said at the time of the film's release that Buddhism teaches that it takes 10,000 years for a soul to evolve to its next level, and that he assumed that was how long Phil is trapped in his loop. I couldn't last that long, reliving that day, over and over; I'd go mad. At what point do you think your sanity would snap? At what point might you give up on ethics and morality when you realised your actions have no consequences? You might think that you could assert joy in every second of your relived existence in such circumstances, but that groundhog isn't going to snare *me* in its Nietzschean nightmare.

Tokyo to rubble, tornadoes rip Los Angeles to pieces and the British Royal Family die when the sudden drop in temperature causes the helicopters transporting them to Balmoral to freeze in mid-air and crash. Jack treks across the newly frozen wasteland to find his son, stuck in an ice-locked New York. The going, we might say, is Ragnaröcky.

It's an entertaining movie, but daft: the temperature, one character declares, is 'dropping 10 degrees a minute!' which would, if true, get us to absolute zero in less than half an hour. One scene that has particularly stayed with me sees Jack's son Sam (Jake Gyllenhaal) literally pursued by the drop in temperature – he and his friends run as the floor freezes behind them as if it is chasing after them, reaching the safety of a room and shutting the door just in time. But it's mean-spirited to sneer – the film is not a documentary, and the vivid special effects are good at conveying the immediacy of its topic.

Climate change is a real and present danger. If you don't believe that then I don't know what to tell you. The scientific consensus on this fact is irrefutable, short of there being a massive international conspiracy by scientists to fool the world. But the idea that a legion of geeks is slowly accumulating forged data and publishing it

6

THE WORLD ON FIRE:
CLIMATE ARMAGEDDON

In Roland Emmerich's environmental disaster movie *The Day After Tomorrow* (2004), the charismatic climate scientist Jack Hall (Dennis Quaid) realises that a massive and catastrophic climate shift is about to strike the world. The authorities refuse to heed his warnings, but he's proven right when a colossal storm system batters the whole of the northern hemisphere, sucking frozen air into more temperate zones and instantly freezing the whole world: a huge hailstorm smashes in obscure academic journals in order to reduce the profits of gigantic petrochemical corporations seems a little far-fetched.

We can be honest: the climate is warming and we are mostly responsible. Some people might point to the natural fluctuations of our climate over time, but the rapid global changes we are seeing at the moment are unprecedented and not comparable with anything that has happened before. Its effects will bring extreme weather events, rising sea levels and increasing temperatures, rendering parts of the world uninhabitable. This statement is probably enough on its own to explain why it is becoming the dominant imaginary for the apocalypse, both in fiction and reality. And in the way it is represented, non-fiction accounts vie with fictional ones in terms of impact and terror.

Edward Struzik's *Firestorm: How Wildfire Will Shape Our Future* (2017) speaks alarmingly of a future dominated by 'megafires', as global temperatures rise, forests become drier and lightning strikes become more common. Warmer temperatures mean longer fire seasons, which in turn release more carbon into the atmosphere, increasing temperatures further. As an example, Struzik discusses the Horse River Fire, which tore through 1.5 million acres of inhabited land in Alberta,

Canada, in 2016. Known by locals as 'the Beast', it turned 2,500 homes and 12,000 vehicles to ash, and forced 90,000 residents to evacuate. 'The firestorm was of such ferocity,' says Struzik, 'it created its own weather patterns, including lightning strikes that set off smaller fires to herald its approach.' More recently, bush fires in Australia began burning in September 2019 and grew more and more severe. By March 2020, when the authorities finally got the situation under control, a staggering 46 million acres had burnt, destroying 6,000 buildings, killing dozens of humans and an astonishing 1 billion animals. Somewhere, John of Patmos is nodding his head sagely.

The problem started some time ago. Since the Industrial Revolution in the eighteenth century, humans have been increasingly polluting the planet as the consumption of fossil fuels took off in earnest. At the time, few people noticed or concerned themselves with the effect on the environment, focusing their apocalyptic anxieties on a different fear: overpopulation. The increase in food production had led to a rapid growth in population that some felt was unsustainable. Of particular influence were the ideas of Thomas Malthus, an eighteenth-century British writer who calculated that population growth would *always* outpace food supply, resulting in starvation on a mass scale for the poorest in society. His controversial theories encouraged some to think the suffering of the poor inevitable, even divinely sanctioned.*

It is a mistake to insist that the global problem is 'overpopulation' – indeed, China's one-child policy made an important dent in that vast country's burgeoning population without reducing the country's carbon pollution. Some might even point instead to the global dropping birth rates, combined with the pressures of an ageing society, as being more likely to threaten our societies. Still, concerns regarding overpopulation and the future of our species don't necessarily track the science. It's a fear that often informs popular culture.

Take *Soylent Green* (1973), the cult film directed by Richard Fleischer and starring Charlton Heston, based on Harry Harrison's novel *Make Room! Make*

---

* Malthus, an Anglican clergyman as well as a social and economic theorist, believed that the disproportion between 'hyperbolic' population growth and 'linear' growth in the capacities of food production was imposed on us by God, to teach virtuous behaviour – by which he meant chastity and restraint: 'the superior power of population,' he wrote, can only be addressed by two things: 'moral restraint' or 'vice and misery'.

Room! (1966). The movie is markedly different to the novel.* Harrison's overpopulation fable concentrates on the degradation of urban life. It is set in 1999, in a run-down New York so overcrowded that people have to share their apartments with strangers. For everyone except the super-rich, food is no longer delicious and varied; most people subsist upon a product made of soya beans and lentils called 'soylent'. The plot of the novel is more or less inconsequential, but Harrison's proposed solution to the problem of global overpopulation is the dissemination of contraception. In the last scene in the novel, the year 2000 begins and a big screen in Times Square announces, 'Census says United States had biggest year ever, end-of-the-century, 344 million citizens!'† It's almost an anticlimax.

Adapting this novel into a movie, the screenwriter Stanley R. Greenberg made a number of changes (including excising all mention of contraception to avoid alienating Roman Catholic cinemagoers), and

---

* Not least in its title, which sounds like an order to add an extension to your house.

† When Harrison was writing, the population of the USA was 200 million, so this number presumably seemed terrifyingly inflated. At the time of my writing, the USA is home to 328 million people, without any signs of collapse.

added a new twist ending that has become the most famous part of the whole story. In the movie, Charlton Heston's character comes to a grisly realisation: far from being made from soya and lentils, 'Soylent Green' is in fact made from processed human corpses. The film ends with the dramatic climax of a horrified Heston staggering through the city streets, warning his fellow New Yorkers: 'Soylent Green is people!'

It's certainly a dramatically effective ending, but it's not a concept that survives a few seconds of rational thought. Soya and lentils are easy to grow and to convert into nutritious food; human beings are neither of those things, never mind the added expense required in keeping it a secret from the general population. But, of course, we should not judge *Soylent Green* in terms of its logical plausibility any more than we should *The Day After Tomorrow*. Its celebrated ending is, on the contrary, a symbolic articulation of a great truth: that we are hungrily consuming our world, devouring our means of subsistence and poisoning our reservoir of resources. The unsustainability is the point. *Soylent Green* is a metaphorical articulation of environmental disaster. We are Monty Python's Black Knight, gaily lopping off our own limbs while loudly boasting about our invincibility.

While we're unlikely to be tricked into eating each other, the question of how we're going to feed our growing population while climate change challenges our existing practices of production and consumption is a valid one. But the problem isn't simply that there are more people alive than ever before; the real issue is that those people are no longer content to live primitive, subsistence-level lives. They want the trappings of modernity: central heating (or air conditioning), internet access, cars, air travel, out-of-season fruit. As climate scientists remind us, around each person exists a circle of influence much larger than the individual – I'm talking, of course, about our 'carbon footprint'. It is the amount of carbon that we've pumped into the atmosphere, through the burning of fossil fuels to power our lifestyle that is the biggest culprit, although there are certainly other problematic industries and practices, from fast fashion to cattle farming.

If we carry on in this way, the consequences will likely be dire. The work of thousands of scientists feeds into the reports issued, periodically, by the UN Intergovernmental Panel on Climate Change (IPCC); most recently the 2018 *Special Report on Global Warming of 1.5°C*. It outlines the warning that unless we cut our carbon emissions significantly over the next two decades to limit the temperature rise to 1.5 degrees above pre-industrial levels by 2100, we will likely start to see heatwaves of magnitudes never experienced by humans, with deaths in the tens and perhaps hundreds of thousands. It might mean the extinction of nearly half of all plant and animal species; agricultural yields would collapse and many millions would starve;* sea levels could rise by more than two metres, submerging entire cities.

Some would say it's already too late. Climate change is already happening, and all of our efforts will only succeed in limiting or delaying the damage. Consequently, research is being conducted into how science and technology might provide more extreme methods of intervention in the form of climate engineering – finding ways of managing solar radiation, for example, or removing greenhouse gases from the atmosphere. Such stories of science saving the day are reassuring – many of our visions of the apocalypse, as we have seen, push things to the brink of disaster, and even beyond, but

---

* In *Don't Even Think About It: Why Our Brains Are Wired to Ignore Climate Change* (2014), George Marshall estimates that if the global temperature were to rise by 4 degrees by 2100, crops would fail across the board in Africa and 'US production of corn, soy beans and cotton would fall by up to 82 per cent'. The 2018 IPCC report can be read here: https://www.ipcc.ch/sr15/

reserve a 'eucatastrophe' or unexpected escape or happy ending – but it seems foolish to *rely* upon such a *deus ex machina* in real life.*

The idea of climate change engineering is also a controversial one, partly because it suggests that we don't need to engage in a systematic overhaul of our lives to address the underlying problem. Another, possibly valid, concern is that we would rush headlong into a scheme intended to save us but that has terrible unforeseen consequences and side effects that only make it worse or create an entirely new problem. Such a scenario is the basis for Bong Joon Ho's movie *Snowpiercer* (2013), a powerfully eloquent portrayal of human hubris in which an attempt to reverse global warming has instead brought on a new ice age, and the last human survivors live on a train that travels endlessly around a frozen world.

The film also focuses on the clash between the lower classes at the tail of the train and the first-class

* The *deus ex machina*, or 'god out of the machine', is a phrase from ancient Greek and Roman drama, where a dramatist would tie up all the loose ends of his complicated plotline by having a god lowered from a special theatrical crane (the 'machine') and disposing of the story with a wave of the divine hand. The climate emergency won't be solved so simply, I fear. It will involve a lot of work, and – yes – a lot of money. We could be looking, in other words, at a 'pay-us' *ex machina*. I can't and won't apologise for this pun.

passengers at the front, and so highlights another very real issue in the climate apocalypse: the fear that the poor will be left to die or scrabble to survive while the wealthy are able to protect themselves from the worst of the effects. We can already see this to some extent: the richest 10 per cent of the population is responsible for more than half of the world's carbon emissions, but are able to protect themselves from the worst effects – they can simply jet off elsewhere when the weather gets a bit extreme. Meanwhile, billions of the poorest people around the world, who tend to have the smallest carbon footprint, are most likely to suffer from climate change – drought, floods and extreme storms. As the effects are felt more keenly, this gap between rich and poor may only widen.

The situation we find ourselves in is understandably scary to most people. Fears over climate change are rising, as is a belief that something must be done – recent Pew Research Center polling finds a 68 per cent global average of the population who consider climate change a serious challenge, rising to as high as 90 per cent in Greece.* But are we scared enough? Given how

* https://www.pewresearch.org/fact-tank/2019/04/18/a-look-at-how-people-around-the-world-view-climate-change/

gloomy the scientific forecasts are – and that this is the one apocalypse scenario it would be quite sensible to be afraid of – perhaps the global figure should be higher, and action should already be well underway. Environmental concerns have been around for decades, after all.

There are reasons why we've been slow on the uptake. Certain groups with a vested interest in the continued use of fossil fuels have lobbied determinedly to obscure or undermine the science and prevent policy changes in regard to energy sources. It might also be more plausibly argued that scientists had difficulty mastering the channels of media communication – years in a lab do not ready a person for the bright lights of a TV studio. At the same time, there is a convention that media coverage must be 'balanced'. With politics this makes sense; it wouldn't be fair for a left-wing pundit to dominate the airwaves without giving a right-wing pundit the chance to reply and rebut, and vice versa. But climate change is about science first and politics only insofar as politicians need to act on what the science determines. We don't look to balance a news story about a new Earth-orbiting satellite with a rebuttal by a flat-earther, or a report about the particle accelerator at CERN with a vox pop by a man who thinks electricity is little demons running up and down copper wire. But for years climate change deniers were given equal footing, even though scientists have been largely in agreement for quite some time. So if the scientists failed initially to communicate the urgency of the situation to the masses, perhaps it's not entirely their fault.

Now, climate change often dominates the headlines. There are still deniers but the global climate strikes, protests and movements demonstrate that people are increasingly getting the message. Even with this raised awareness, however, scientists agree that not nearly enough is being done to avert the crisis. According to the IPCC report mentioned above, to avoid the worst-case scenarios we need to limit the global rise in temperature to 1.5 degrees by 2100. On our current trajectory, we could be looking at a rise of between 2 and 4 degrees in that time.

At the heart of our stories, real and fictional, is a warning of what is to come if we do not confront the problem head-on. Because while we might very sensibly fear climate change itself, what we should really be afraid of is our own apathy and inaction. Climate change is not just a story on our screens, nor are we unfortunate victims of an unavoidable fate. This is not a fictional invasion of the undead, a rogue crazed general pressing the red button, or the Sun engulfing us in a billion years. We are the ones driving it; we are doing this to ourselves. And only we can change that.

There certainly are actions we can still take to reduce our impact on our environment and avoid the most catastrophic effects of global warming – from transforming our methods of food production and diets to ceasing large-scale clearances of forests and investing heavily in renewable energy while keeping fossil fuels in the ground – requiring the combined efforts of individuals, governments and corporations across the world. So why are we still finding it so difficult to get to grips with this?

Perhaps we are simply overwhelmed by the scale and severity of the problem combined with the complexity of coordinating global efforts in overhauling our way of life. The fear of how daunting the task is has paralysed us into inaction. Some people are already throwing their hands up in defeat, claiming there is nothing we can do. Yet this eco trauma seems to be having an influence on the environmental dialogue; stories are emerging that focus less on panic and catastrophe and more on providing solutions. The Australian documentary film 2040 (directed by Damon Gameau, 2019), for example, envisions a future in which climate change has been solved using the technology available to us today. Its optimistic message is intended to provide hope and inspiration, a call to action.

One of the reasons Gene Roddenberry's Star Trek franchise has endured so well, with multiple TV serials, movies, tie-in novelisations, video games, reboots and spin-offs from its inception in 1966 right up to the present day, is the way it offers fans a positive vision of future possibilities. According to the fictional 'timeline' that lies behind the show's twenty-third-century spacefaring and utopian Federation, the middle decades of the twenty-first century saw a general collapse on earth due to war and environmental degradation. Only when humankind had sunk so low was it possible to come together and rebuild a harmonious and rejuvenated world.*

---

* *Star Trek* is almost unique, I think, in representing climate apocalypse as something that happened in the past, and which humanity overcame by collective action. Whenever the twenty-fourth-century earth is portrayed, it is a utopian blend of harmonious pastoral and urban stylings. Yet in 'Future's End', a double episode of *Star Trek: Voyager* from 1996, a Federation starship is thrown back in time and we learn that in 2047 California was flooded due to climate change. In the *Star Trek: The Next Generation* episode 'True Q' (1992), we discover that in the late twenty-first century, humanity worked together to find a scientific fix for the world-spanning tornadoes climate change had thrown up. Most famously perhaps, the whole story of the motion picture *Star Trek IV: The Voyage Home* (1986) concerns rescuing the last whales from extinction.

Nevertheless, many of our climate apocalypse stories still tend to play more on our fears. There are those that handle it more thoughtfully and accurately, as in Kim Stanley Robinson's scrupulously researched and carefully worked-through 'Science in the Capital' trilogy,* a near-future extrapolation of today's climate change trajectories into a plausibly written near future that highlights the urgency of the situation – many of the characters are scientists, and they are not shy about explaining to other characters the various implications of climate science. But many more prefer to throw science to the wind in a melodramatic fashion. Writers and filmmakers need to inject excitement and narrative thrills into what is not, in its purely environmental-science sense, a very exciting story. A vitally important story, don't get me wrong, but a slow, aggregative and encroaching story, rather than a sharply delineated good-guys/bad-guys rollercoaster of the kind Hollywood prefers.

Contemporary culture mimics contemporary society: caffeinated and sugar-high, often pepped up with drugs, our society has been so bombarded by

---

* *Forty Signs of Rain* (2004), *Fifty Degrees Below* (2005) and *Sixty Days and Counting* (2007).

stimulants we have developed a tolerance that can only be overcome by ever-higher stimulation. Our culture, today, *is* a hyperstimulant. Climate change is poorly served by such an agitated and agitating popular discourse, but it can be hard to grab people's attention any other way.

People understand immediate threats – the image of ice sprinting across the floor after the protagonists in *The Day After Tomorrow* is a very clear and present danger. The reality of climate change is that it is gradual and therefore people don't necessarily grasp the urgency, even if they understand the importance. Although the effects are already on display, they are being felt unequally around the globe. We can all gasp at the images of Australia on fire, but it is not the same as it happening to *you*. Most people are not yet seriously suffering the consequences. And so a warning of ten years seems deferrable, and a warning of a hundred years might as well be a million. What doesn't filter through is that solving the problem is also a slow process, that we need to take measures now as they will only have an effect over time. As the writer William Gibson astutely remarked on Twitter, 'We've never had a cultural model for an apocalypse that lasts for a century or two. We don't even know how to make a movie or a pop song about such a slow catastrophe.'*

The environmental campaigner George Marshall conceptualises climate change 'as the ultimate challenge to our ability to make sense of the world around us. More than any other issue it exposes the deepest workings of our minds, and shows our extraordinary and innate talent for seeing only what we want to see and disregarding what we would prefer not to know.'[†] According to Marshall, our failure to act is a result not of a lack of knowledge or of political will, but of our inability to grasp what is going on. We are presently not acting in a way equal to the reality because that would mean acknowledging that it is actually happening. The problem, in other words, is that the crisis is *environmental*. Our environment is what surrounds us, we are immersed in it, and that's what makes it so hard to see. We can allow ourselves to ignore the problem and let it fade into the background and into the future.

So, although we are afraid of climate change in theory, in our minds it is an issue that doesn't yet directly

---

*   @GreatDismal, 25 August 2019.
[†]   George Marshall, *Don't Even Think About It: Why Our Brains Are Wired to Ignore Climate Change* (Bloomsbury, 2014), p. 2.

affect many of us in the Western world and therefore is not prioritised over issues that are pressing right now. Fear of change and disruption, having to give up the luxuries we have come to rely on and enjoy, outweighs the fear of a threat that is down the line. One of the arguments against transforming the way we live, for example, is the economic hardships many people would suffer. In fact, many reports suggest that there would be plenty of economic benefits – job creation and improvement for our physical and mental health, for example. But even if the closure of certain industries, such as coal, isn't balanced by the creation of new green technologies, we should not take the short-sighted approach; we have to factor in the harm suffered by future generations. This is called 'stewardship' and it is one of the human responsibilities that undergird and validate our human rights (for there are no rights without responsibilities). Stewardship, though, is hard, and requires us to think of others as well as ourselves. It is easier to pretend that it's not going to happen, or that science will swoop in and save us at the last moment. Eighteenth-century Irish politician Boyd Roche is reputed to have asked during parliamentary debate, 'Why we should put ourselves out of our way to do anything for posterity, for what has posterity ever done for us?' People laughed at Boyd Roche, and rightly so. We don't want to be like Boyd Roche. But it is an attitude that is still discernible in certain parts of the climate discourse.

Certainly in the past we've never been that good at looking after the world around us. We've taken our planet for granted, and in doing so, in focusing on our immediate needs and self-interest, we allowed some of our worst traits to run rampant. We are used to exploiting our planet and its resources. It has become second nature to put ourselves first without thinking of the longer-term consequences, stretching back to the days when our ancestors hunted the woolly mammoth to extinction. But it is a modern invention that best encapsulates this attitude: videogames. Fictional worlds where there are no consequences, where nothing matters, and everything exists to serve the player.

There's been a huge surge in immersive videogames in modern times. As gaming has grown in popularity through the twenty-first century to the point where it is arguably the most vibrant and widespread form of popular culture, the games that have enjoyed the greatest success have been ones that create a 3D world in which players explore and engage with their virtual environments. The world's biggest-selling single game, *Minecraft*, has sold 200 million copies since 2011, and it is *all* environment, a virtual space in which first-person-point-of-view players dig, build, explore and fight other players. Other immersive game franchises have earned staggering sums of money: the *Call of Duty* series (several of which are set in explorable Second World War worlds, although later games have been set in other historical periods) has earned $17 billion globally. And the *World of Warcraft* games, in which you explore a high fantasy world with other players, has earned $10 billion and generated successful spin-off TV shows and movies.

The core logic of these games is that the world and everything in it is a means to an end, and you should always treat it like that. And it is this attitude, reified into a system of real-world belief, that is fuelling the ongoing climate catastrophe through which we are living.

A few years ago, the English novelist Will Self 'hung out' with his teenage son as he played a series of video games, in an attempt to bond with him, including *Skyrim*, in which players explore a fantasy world, acquiring items and weapons, killing monsters and fighting other players:

Eventually, once we had defeated various frost trolls and sex-changing lizard men, and reached Windhelm, it transpired that my son had built a gabled house in this Arctic community, and even acquired a wife. 'My wife is a very nice lady,' he told me, as a rather cowed-looking figure in a rough woollen dress shuffled about in the background. 'She runs a store and gives me money every few days.' 'Oh, really,' I said, desperate to clutch at these straws of domesticity. 'And what's your wife's name?' Without pausing in the ceaseless toggling of thumb-on-lever he said: 'I don't know.'*

That last exchange, and its hilarious pay-off, gets to the heart of the matter: video games are based on the idea that everything *and everybody* is a resource for you to exploit in the furtherance of your gameplay. It is good to have a wife, insofar as it leads to gameplay advantage.

The cornerstone of Immanuel Kant's ethical philosophy is that we should always treat other people as ends in themselves rather than as merely means to an end. Terry Pratchett advances the same moral argument in his many Discworld novels. In *Carpe Jugulum* (1998), a character describes sin as 'when you treat people as things. Including yourself.' And when Immanuel Kant

---

* Will Self, 'Video Games', *London Review of Books*, 8 November 2012: https://www.lrb.co.uk/v34/n21/will-self/diary

and Terry Pratchett agree on something, it seems to me a very good reason for thinking it true.

Video games of course have nothing directly to do with climate change (beyond the creation and use of billions of computers and the generation of the electricity to run them). But the way these games have developed is symbolic of this exploitative attitude with which we approach everything, including our planet. Climate change is a result of us treating the world as a resource that we should exploit rather than a life-support system to nurture, and often doing so in a wholly unconsidered way, as if killing it wholesale is the most natural thing in the world.

I see one contemporary narrative above all others as the most purely representative of our ongoing environmental apocalypse: the *Dark Souls* video game trilogy. The first volume appeared in 2011, with the second and third instalments following in 2014 and 2016.

In *Dark Souls* you are in charge of a character that moves around an intricately detailed, enormous, ruinous gothic fantasy world. There are many separate realms, all linked to one another, and all to varying degrees broken, collapsed, burnt out and desertified. But where other first-person adventure games ramp up excitement via a fast-paced, kinetic and often brightly coloured environment, the world of *Dark Souls* is relentlessly downbeat, dour and underlit. Everything is the colour of ashes and shadows. There is little by way of ambient music, although from time to time doomy orchestral music swells in the aural background. Mostly the only sound is that of your own footsteps, echoing through ruined castles or claustrophobic valleys, or the slash of weapons cutting into flesh. The visual design is extremely beautiful in a mournful, collapsed sort of way, but there is something mind-boggling about the sheer *relentlessness* of this imagined world – it's a potent and often repellent mixture of the decayed and the actively ugly. When vitality bursts into the gameplay, it might be because some enemy has sprouted from a swordsman into a huge, tentacular mass of hideousness, an apotheosis of deformity. There are various storylines, but the fundamental battle concerns the question of whether to try to renew the world, or to league oneself with the Darkstalker Kaathe, let the fire that sustains humanity die out altogether and bring about a terminal Age of Dark.

It is the perfect artwork for the Anthropocene, and not just because video games have become so extraordinarily popular nowadays. Games provides players with choices, but those choices are in many ways illusions – the possible outcomes are limited to those created by the game's designer to fit their intended story structure. In real life our options are similarly constrained – not by a 'game designer', but by the choices previous generations made with respect to our environment.

Nevertheless, we do still have choices available to us that can change the direction of our story. And we have proved that we are able to take decisive action when it is needed. For example: when it became apparent in the late 1970s that the ozone layer was being degraded by chlorofluorocarbons and other man-made chemicals, international cooperation led to the Montreal Protocol of 1987 restricting their use and emission. Ozone levels stabilised by the mid 1990s and began to recover in the 2000s. Similar stories can be told when it comes to endangered animal species, and rolling back the industrial pollution of rivers.* But there is a lot to do, and we as a species need to find the resolve to do what is necessary. Our fears for the future of our planet are valid. But we don't have to accept that fate. The climate challenge can be overcome if we fully abandon our long-established extractive, exploitative attitude.

* A good account of these kinds of victories is Frank M. Dunnivant's *Environmental Success Stories: Solving Major Ecological Problems and Confronting Climate Change* (Columbia University Press, 2017).

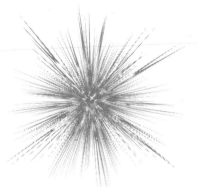

EPILOGUE

THE END IS NEVER

The end of the world is ever on our minds. As we've seen, popular culture is busy with predictions and visions of our own demise, from religious myths to video games, from journalism to science fiction. Our fascination with the end times has created a remarkable array of apocalyptic subgenres, by turns baleful and strangely emancipatory – machine uprisings, zombie swarms, alien annihilations. Each story is revealing in its own way, but collectively they say something far more significant about humanity.

Sometimes what these stories say is quite straight-forward: that the actual end of the world scares us. It's very possible that climate change will render our planet uninhabitable, or that an asteroid will come hurtling through space to obliterate us. It's not unreasonable to fear these things. I started this book by looking into Bayesian probability calculations that suggest that the end of the world is coming much sooner than we might think. The Doomsday Clock, created in 1947, is a representation of how close we could be to the final curtain: the threat level portrayed by the number of minutes to midnight – the moment of final catastrophe. When it was set up, that number was seven minutes; now, thanks to the escalating dangers of climate change and nuclear conflict, it is just 100 seconds. We do seem to be living through interesting times.

But is this the sort of end we mean when we're exploring the end of the world in our storytelling? In reality, most of the ways we portray Armageddon are unlikely to come about any time soon: the gods seem unwilling or unable to destroy their creation; the sun has a few more billion years of fuel to burn; disease can be devastating – something we're very aware of in a world shaken by Covid-19 – but not world-ending. The chance of all life being extinguished in one dramatic event seems small. It is more likely that we'll slowly dwindle away – but then there is always something to take our place. Other people carry on when we die; other species may evolve in our place; other planets will continue to exist without Earth. Like the Eternal Return, an end comes; the end never does. Perhaps, in fact, the end of the world is not nigh. Perhaps it is never.

When it comes to the apocalypse, however, we're not really worried about the end of the world. We're worried about the end of *our* world. Individual mortality is clearly a theme that runs through apocalyptic fiction – as we've seen, we project our anxieties over our own death onto the world. Earlier I discussed H. G. Wells's visions of how the world might end – the hammer blow from on high that is *The War of the Worlds*, and the gathering entropic gloom of the universal heat death in *The Time Machine*. His very last book, written decades later when he himself was an old and decrepit man, is called *Mind at the End of Its Tether* (1945) and takes a different approach again. Barely a book, it is more like a pamphlet: thirty-four pages and eight short chapters. Written as he was dying, and published after his death, it is an unremittingly pessimistic prediction of the inevitable end of humanity.

This is easily the strangest thing Wells ever wrote. From his deathbed, he relays a sudden insight he has had that everything is approaching its end 'within a period to be estimated by weeks and months rather than by aeons'. Something about the cosmos has suddenly and profoundly altered: 'There has been a fundamental change in the conditions under which life, not simply human life but all self-conscious existence, has been going on since its beginning.' If his thinking has been 'sound', he says, 'then this world is at the end of its tether. The end of everything we call life is close at hand and cannot be evaded.' *Homo sapiens* is 'played out' – 'The stars in their courses have turned against him and he has to give place to some other animal.' *Mind at the End of Its Tether* offers no hard evidence for Wells's strange presentiment that everything was coming to an end; it simply keeps returning to the idea that a nameless something is bringing doom. Of course, what had changed in Wells's world was the awareness of his own imminent end.

It is something we still do today, imagining the end over and over again, in a compulsive loop of disaster clichés, as we continue to struggle collectively with the knowledge of our own inevitable deaths. And in a sense, that is the end of the world; from an individual perspective, the world only exists because we are in it. Without that perspective, the world is lost when we are.

The apocalypse is not simply a conceptualising of death, collective or individual. Which is to say, it is that, but not *only* that. These stories also explore our insecurities about the world and our place in it. There seem to be many precarious aspects to the situation humanity finds itself in: fragile societies that could collapse into chaos at any moment; the insignificance of our lonely planet circling one of trillions of stars in a universe that is unfathomably large; our own human nature, which so often seems set to self-destruct. Through our stories we have constructed a version of the world that gives an illusion of security – one made out of societies, laws, religions. But that world of our creation is vulnerable to change and upheaval; even though physically it might not end, those structures can, and have, come crashing down. Imagining the end of the world is an expression of our collective anxiety over life as well as death.

We use these stories to make sense of it all, to impose order on an uncaring and chaotic universe, creating the fantasy that we have some measure of understanding and control. This is not something that the universe engages in. The Big Bang is not a story – it just is (or was). Gravity and entropy do not have some grand significance beyond their existence and function. The cosmos, after all, is under no obligation to make sense to us.

Nevertheless, we look to fictions to add meaning and structure to our experience, and our storytelling tradition is based upon a linear progression: beginning, middle and end. For us to derive any meaning from the story, we have to know how it will end. For example, many people read the Bible as a linear story about the world as a whole, one with a beginning (Genesis), middle (now) and an end (Revelation). And that is also how we tend to understand our own stories: birth, life, death. Knowing how our story ends would give us the chance to consider our own lives and mortality, to make sense of our place in time and work out what is meaningful about our lives. And so stories of the end are not about a particular event, though they purport to be. They're about how we all live all the time. The end is only the *frame* of our life; what matters is what that frame contains – connection, meaning, living.

One of the most fertile ideas the critic Frank Kermode floats in his influential book *The Sense of an*

Ending is the distinction he draws between two kinds of time. One type he calls *chronos*, ordinary time that passes as one second per second; the other is *kairos*, a more transcendent and sublime kind of time. *Chronos* consists of all the ordinary moments with which our lives are filled but have no importance; they are routine actions that do not truly capture the human experience. *Kairos* are the points in time filled with significance that tell us who we are; the exciting and pivotal moments of our existence, charged with meaning.

We experience both *chronos* and *kairos* simultaneously, but we must live in *chronos*, in the normal progression of time. This can be fine, as we go about our lives, but we can come to feel that we are trapped in the tedium of the everyday. On the other hand, we are drawn to *kairos* – the *right* time, the special and magical time – but we can't live that way twenty-four hours a day, seven days a week. Worse, it can be hard even discerning which are the truly important occasions in life. As in any story, their meaning is derived from their relation to the end.

But what could be more exciting and meaningful than the end itself? The ending is a key part of the story, we want to play a part in it, to be the heroes – not some insignificant character killed off prematurely. If humanity keeps on going thousands of years after our deaths, what was the point of our lives in the grander scheme of things? We are enticed by apocalypse because its arrival would make our time in the world more special. This is why people who predict the real-life end of the world place it imminently, within their own lifetime, and why most of those predictions aren't really about the end but about times of transcendence and rebirth – capturing a moment of *kairos* that will last forever.

Most of us aren't walking down the street wearing placards proclaiming the end is nigh. Instead we resort to our stories of disaster to explore our desire to escape the mundanity of life – imagining the starring role we could play, how the story of humanity unfolds, what it would be like to reduce the boredom of our everyday routines to one exciting purpose: survival. And so the reason why we are so drawn to the end, however grimly it is envisioned, is because we are tantalised by the gleam of wonder that *kairos* casts upon our humdrum lives.

The struggle to find meaning in our lives, the need to place ourselves at the centre of the story, is only natural. Our own life, our own experiences, are the only frames of reference that we have for existence. This is why the idea of the world carrying on beyond our deaths is so troubling, and why ultimately it's impossible for us to imagine the end – ours or the world's – through to its conclusion.

Our storytelling can only take us so far in making sense of our lives, because it is based in the idea of the lived experience. And since death is not lived through, by definition, it is not 'experienced' as another thing that happens day-to-day. We have no way to imagine ourselves as not existing. When we try and frame mortality and finality as a story, something in our mind rebels.

In reality what we envision is not really the end. As we've seen during the course of this book, humanity is forever creating loopholes, survivors, rebirths and trapdoors that enable us to skip away from the ultimate end of things and start anew. It's almost as if the only way we can make sense of an ending is through new beginnings. We are trapped in linear time, but we also encounter time in cycles and recurrences: days, years, seasons. We watch the leaves fall from the trees in autumn, only to return again in spring. Life ebbs and flows.

If we cannot truly experience the moment of death, perhaps the end really is never. The universe, as we saw in Chapter 5, will most likely slowly decline into increasingly dark and chilly entropy, forever approaching and never quite reaching the parabolic flatness of ultimate end. Perhaps that is also how we will experience death – like a form of Zeno's paradoxes, it is an end destination we can never truly arrive at. Of course it will 'happen', but not for us, not for our minds and consciousness. In the sense of lived experience, death will never arrive. Not only is 'the end' not nigh, it is impossible.

In September 1919, towards the end of the war to end all wars, Franz Kafka published a short story called 'An Imperial Message'. It is a very *short* short story, barely a page long, although I think it is also one of the best things he ever wrote. As he was writing it, everything was falling apart in his world. He lived in Prague, one of the major cities of the soon-to-be-defeated Austro-Hungarian empire. The old emperor, Franz Joseph, had died late in 1916 at the age of eighty-six, having ruled since 1848. Towards the end of his reign, his citizens could no longer remember a time when he hadn't been emperor and it began to seem that he would go on forever. But eventually he did die, and the Austro-Hungarian empire was dismantled just two months after Kafka's story was written. This is how 'An Imperial Message' begins:

The Emperor – they say – sent a message, dictated it from his death bed, sent it to you alone, his feeble subject, to that miniature shadow hiding at the remotest distance from the imperial sun. He instructed the messenger to kneel down beside his bed and whisper the message in his ear. It was important, he believed, to get the messenger to repeat it back to him. He confirmed the messenger's accuracy by nodding his head.

And so the messenger heads off with his message. It is to us that it is directed, but before he can reach us, he must make his way from the emperor's deathbed, through the crowd of people attending the imperial passing. Then he has to make his way out of the huge palace, passing through an interminable number of chambers and antechambers. If it had been a matter, Kafka says, of simply crossing an open field he would have made rapid progress, but as it is, things are hopeless:

> He is still making his way through all the private rooms of the inner palace. He will never find a way through. And even if he did, it wouldn't make any difference. He'd only have to struggle down the

palace steps, and, even if he did that, it wouldn't make any difference. He'd still have the courtyards to cross, and after the courtyards the second palace that encircles the first, and, again, down stairs and through courtyards, and then, yet again, another palace, and so on for millennia. But say he managed at last to burst through the outermost door – although such a thing could never, never happen – why then: the whole royal capital city, the centre of the world, is standing before him, heaped buildings and streets clogged with mud. No one forces his way through such a place, certainly not a man carrying a message from a dead man.

The message, clearly, will never reach us. This is the final line of Kafka's story: 'But nevertheless, you sit at your window as evening falls, and you dream the message to yourself.' In its gorgeous, haunting obliqueness this has always seemed to me one of Kafka's most accomplished short stories. The end of the story never quite reaches us; we are left to imagine it for ourselves.

Our fascination with the end is always a contradiction. We feel death gives life meaning, we know it is inevitable and we are drawn to the excitement the end promises; but at the same time we cannot accept or understand the reality of it. We especially don't want anything to end in the chaotic, unresolved way the universe might impose upon us. And so we continue to imagine it, over and over, in our search for meaning, for a moment of transcendence; a way to transform its finality into an experience we can finally comprehend.

INDEX

28 Days Later film 62
666, number of the Beast 49–50, 52
2040 documentary 168–9

A

afterlife, imagining an 10–11
AIDS 101–3
Aldiss, Brian 63–4
alien intelligences and invaders 117–18, 119–24
alien plagues 87–8, 89
Allen, Woody 74
Alzheimer's disease 76
Amis, Martin 102
'An Imperial Message' (F. Kafka) 190–2
Andaman people 32
antibodies and immunity 81–2
The Antiquary (W. Scott) 6
apocalypse insurance 7–8
Apocalypse video game 9
Apollo 79–80
Armageddon film 125–6
asteroid/planet collisions 124–9
Australian bush fires (2019–20) 158
Australians, indigenous 82–3
avian flu 85

B

B612 Foundation 128
The Battle of Dorking (G. T. Chesney) 118–19
Battlestar Galactica TV series 115
Bayes, Thomas 18
Bayesian probability 17–22, 182
Bear, Greg 89
'the Beast' 42–4, 49–50
berserkers in science fiction 114
Biblical apocalypse 8–9, 15, 39–52
Big Bang theory 137–8
    as infinitely repeated event 150–4
    process reversal 143–4
Big Bounce 144, 150, 151–4
Big Crunch 144, 149–50
bioengineering 70
bioweapons 84, 86
Black Death 81, 92
Black Lives Matter movement 60–1
Black Sea 30–1
Blackwood's Magazine 118
Blood Music film 89
bodily and mental decay 73–7
bodily decay, fear of 73–7
Bonaparte, Napoleon 52
Bong Joon Ho 164
'The Book of the New Sun' (G. Wolfe) 148

The Botanic Garden (E. Darwin)
146–7
Boyle, Danny 62
Brave New World (A. Huxley) 68–9
Buddhism 23, 154
Bunyan, John 12–13
burial practices 74–5
Byron, Lord 6, 93, 94, 98, 139–40,
146

C
Call of Duty video game series 175
Cameron, James 112
carbon footprints/emissions 162,
163, 165
see also climate change
Carpe Jugulum (T. Pratchett) 176
Chernobyl disaster 52–3
Chesterton, G. K. 4–6
Children of Men film 9
Chinese astronomy 33
Chinese one-child policy 159
Christian God *see* God, Christian
Christianity 8–9, 15, 23, 25, 33
chronos and *kairos* concept 187–8
Cioran, Emil 141
'Cities in Flight' novels (J. Blish)
148–9
climate change 27, 182
carbon emissions/carbon
footprints 162, 163, 165
The Day After Tomorrow film
155–6
deniers 166–7
engineering control 163–4
Industrial Revolution 158
negative influence of video
games 174–9
population growth 158–62
portrayal in fiction 155–6, 170–1

speed of human response
166–7, 171–3
stewardship 173–4
taking collective action 168–9,
173–4, 179
wildfire 157–8
cocoliztli epidemic 82
Cold War 108
The Colour Out of Space (H. P.
Lovecraft) 87
comedy in zombie fiction 66–7
consumerism/capitalism and
zombies 64–5, 67–9
Contagion film 80
Copernicus 22
Covid-19 global pandemic (2020)
2, 59, 85, 86, 100, 105–6
creation and uncreation of life
26–9

D
Danse Macabre woodcuts (H.
Holbein) 92–3
dark energy 145
Dark Forest (Liu Cixin) 122–4
Dark Knight film 87
Dark Souls video game 177–8
'Darkness' (Byron) 139–40
Darwin, Erasmus 146–7
Dawn of the Dead film 9, 65
The Day After Tomorrow film
155–6
The Day the Earth Caught Fire film
125
death, human inability to imagine
9–11, 189
death of earth
Big Bang as infinitely repeated
event 150–4
death of the Sun 134–7

entropy of the universe 138–42
eucatasrophe vs tragedy 145–8
influence beyond the Big
    Crunch 149–50
reversal of the Big Bang 143–4
science fiction genre 148–9
The Time Machine (H. G. Wells)
    130–4, 142
Death's End (Liu Cixin) 124
Decameron (Boccaccio) 92
Deep Impact film 126
dementia 76
Dernier Homme (J. de Grainville)
    95
Deucalion 28–9
deus ex machina 164
disease *see* plagues
Divine Incantations Scripture, Taoist
    33–4
Donne, John 4
Don't Even Think About It
    (G. Marshall) 172
'Doom Soon' vs 'Doom Delayed'
    20–2
Doomsday argument 17, 18–22
Doomsday Clock 182
Dr. Strangelove film 15, 108–11
Dracula Unbound film 63–4
dying earth *see* death of earth
Dying Earth (J. Vance) 148

E
Ea 32
earth, death of *see* death of earth
Ebola virus 85
Eddington, Arthur 135–6
Efthimiou, Costas 63
Egypt, Ancient 74–5
Einstein, Albert 135–6
Emmerich, Roland 120–1, 155–6

The End of the World (J. Leslie)
    17
entropy of the universe 138–42
environmental change *see* climate
    change
Environmental Success Stories
    (F. M. Dunnivant) 179
Epic of Gilgamesh 32
'Eternal Return' concept,
    Nietzsche's 151–3, 183
Ethelred, King 52
eucatastrophe vs tragedy 145
European settlers, disease spread
    by 81–3
evangelical Christians 25
extinction events, asteroid 127

F
Fail-Safe (E. Burdick and
    H. Wheeler) 108
Fail Safe film 108–9
falsification, scientific 143
The Female Man film 88
Firestorm (E. Struzik) 157–8
'The Flea' (J. Donne) 100–1
Fleischer, Richard 159–60
floods 28–9, 30–2
four horsemen of the apocalypse
    23, 41
Frankenstein (M. Shelley) 26, 27,
    111
Freud, Sigmund 95–6
front end vs back end of time
    concepts 12–14

G
Gaiman, Neil 15, 39
'Galactic Center' novels
    (G. Benford) 114–15
Gameau, Damon 168–9

Garland, Alex 62
Gay Science (F. Nietzsche) 151
Get Out film 61
Gibson, William 171–2
The Girl with All the Gifts
    (M. R. Carey) 58
global warming *see* climate change
God, Christian 11, 24, 43–4
God, Hebrew 24, 29
gods' inability to uncreate 27–9
Good Omens (T. Prachett and
    N. Gaiman) 15, 39
graphic novels 57
gravity 144–5
Great War 105
Greek mythology 27–9, 79–80
Greeks, Ancient 10, 79–80, 164
Greenberg, Stanley R. 160–1
Groundhog Day film 153–4
Guns, Germs, and Steel
    (J. Diamond) 81

H
Haitian slave plantations 59
Halperin, Victor 59
heat death, universal 138–42,
    153–4, 183
heatwaves, killer 163
heaven, Christian 10
Hebrew Bible 10
Hebrew God *see* God, Hebrew
Hindu mythology 31–2
HIV 85, 101–3
Hobson, Henry 72
Holbein, Hans 92–3
Homer 10, 79–80
Hopi people 38
Horse River Fire, Canada 157–8
Huastec people 32
humour, apocalyptic 14–15

I
Iliad (Homer) 79–80
imperialism, Western 118
Independence Day film 9, 89, 120–1
India 32
Industrial Revolution 158–9
'Inhibitors' series (A. Reynolds) 115
insurance, apocalypse 7–8
invasion stories 118–24
Islam 24, 25
isopsephy 49–50

J
Jaffa, Rick 89–90
Jerusalem, Siege of 45–51
Jesus 11, 25, 33, 44–5, 47–8
Jewish messiah 33, 44, 47
Jones, Duane 61
Josephus 51
Judaism 33, 44–8, 51

K
Kant, Immanuel 176–7
Kermode, Frank 25–6, 186–7
Kirkman, Robert 57
Kubrick, Stanley 15, 108–11

L
The Last Man (M. Shelley) 93–5, 97
Leslie, John 17
Li Hong, Prince 34
Lif and Lifthrasir 37
Liu Cixin 121–4
Love and Death film 74
Lugosi, Bela 59
Lumet, Sidney 108

M
maculae/sunspots 134–5
Maggie film 72–3

Mahdi (end-times messiah) 25
Mahshar Al Qiy'amah 24
Make Room! Make Room!
    (H. Harrison) 159–60
Malthus, Thomas 158–9
Manu 31–2
Marshall, George 163, 172
Martin, John 39
Mass Effect video game 115
Maté, Rudolph 125
Matrix trilogy films 90–1, 115–17
Mayan calendar 3
Melancholia film 126
Mesoamerica 32
Mesopotamia 31, 32
messiah figures 25, 33, 44
    see also Jesus
Meteor film 125–6
Micromégas (Voltaire) 117
The Migration (H. Marshall) 99
Mind at the End of its Tether
    (H. G. Wells) 183–4
Minecraft video game 174–5
*Miscellaneous Discourses Concerning
    the Dissolution and Changes
    of the World* (J. Ray) 134–5
Moore, Tony 57
mortality, human awareness of
    4–6, 184–6
mortality, religion structuring 24

N
Native American people 82
Near East 31
Nero, Emperor 50
Newton, Michael 67
Nietzsche, Friedrich 151–3
The Night Eats the World film 72
The Night Land (W. H. Hodgson)
    147–8

Night of the Living Dead film 56, 61
Noah 29, 31
Nolan, Christopher 87
Norse mythology 9, 34–8
nuclear reactors 26, 52–3
nuclear weapons/holocaust 15, 70,
    107–11

O
Odin 34–5
Old Testament 29
Omen film trilogy 39
Outbreak film 80, 84
overpopulation, global 159–61
ozone levels 179

P
Palawan people 83
pandemic anxiety 84
'Parasitology' trilogy (M. Grant) 70
The Passage trilogy (J. Cronin) 58
Passover 46
Peloponnesian plague 85
pessimism, philosophical 141–2
Physics of Immortality (F. Tipler)
    149–50
Pickens, Slim 109–10
Pitman, Walter 31
Plague Inc. video game 88
plagues 80–1
    alien infections in fiction 87–8,
        89
    Ancient Greece 79–80
    antibodies and immunity 81–2
    assigning agency to 85–90
    Black Death 81, 92
    Covid-19 85, 86, 100, 105–6
    disease spread by European
        settlers 81–3
    freedom from civilisation 95–8

plagues (continued)
  globalisation/
    interconnectedness 83–4, 86
  gothic 19th century portrayal
    93–5
  human sociability 99–100,
    105–6
  humans as plague 90–2
  humans deserving 89–92
  and humans on the same side
    89
  'last man' trope 93–9
  light-hearted portrayal of 92–3
  science fiction 87–90
  and sex 100–3
  Spanish Flu 103–5
  zombies 62–3, 88
Planet of the Apes films 90
plastic pollution 27
Polidori, John William 93
Pompeii 50
Popper, Karl 143
population growth 158–9
Pralaya 31–2
Pratchett, Terry 15, 39, 176–7
Prince, Russ Alan 8
probability, Bayesian 17–22, 182
Prometheus 27–9
Prose Edda (Snorri Sturluson) 37–8
Puluga 32

R
Ragnarök 9, 37
  see also Norse mythology
Ramis, Harold 154
Ray, John 134–5
Red Alert (P. George) 107–8
religion, purpose of 24
religious doomsday 23–4
  belief of imminence 25–6

Book of Revelation 8–9, 15,
  39–54
floods 28–9, 30–2, 34
gods' inability to uncreate 26–9
messiah figures 25, 33–4
Norse mythology 34–8
punishing human sinfulness
  27–30, 31–3, 38
saving the faithful 32–4, 38
valiant defiance of Vikings 34–8
Resident Evil video game and film
  franchise 65
Revelation, Book of 8–9, 15, 39–54
Reyes, Xavier Aldana 71
Rigaut, Jacques 11
Robinson, Kim Stanley 170
Robles, Angelo 7–8
Roche, Boyd 173–4
Rocher, Dominique 72
Roddenberry, Gene 169
Roman Empire 45–6, 48–50, 164
A Romance of Two Worlds
  (M. Corelli) 117
Romero, George A. 9, 56, 61
Russ, Joanna 88
Rutherford, Ernest 135–6
Ryan, William 31
Ryle, John 104

S
Saberhagen, Fred 114
Saint John's Book of Revelation
  8–9, 15, 39–54
Saint Luke 48
Saint Matthew 48
The Satan Bug film 87–8
Schopenhauer, Arthur 142
'Science in the Capital' trilogy
  (K. S. Robinson) 170
Scott, Walter 5–6

'The Screwfly Solution'
(A. Sheldon) 87
Self, Will 175–6
Sellers, Peter 109–10
The Sense of an Ending
(F. Kermode) 186–7
seven suns, Buddhist 23
Seveneves (N. Stephenson) 6–7
sex and plague 100–3
Shaun of the Dead film 66–7
Shelley, Mary 27, 93, 97, 111
Shelley, Percy Bysshe 93
Sheol, Hebrew 10
Shippey, Tom 35–6
Silver, Amanda 90
sinfulness, punishing human
27–30
Skyrim video game 175–6
slavery and racial discrimination
59, 60–1
Smith, Agent (*The Matrix*) 90–1,
116
Snowpiercer film 164–5
social decay and zombies 69–70
Sontag, Susan 103
Soylent Green film 159–61
'Space' trilogy (C. S. Lewis) 117
Spanish Flu 83, 103–5
Sparta 80
Special Report on Global Warming
(IPCC report 2018) 162–3,
167
Spider Woman, Hopi culture's 38
The Stand (S. King) 39
Star Trek 169
Stephenson, Neal 6–7
storytelling and the apocalypse
6–9, 32–4, 38, 145–6, 185–9
Stross, Charlie 59, 60
Sturluson, Snorri 37

Sun, death of the 134–9
'Supper's Ready' (Genesis) 39
survival guides, zombie apocalypse
56
Survivors TV series 84
Sveinsson, Brynjólfur 35

T
Taoism 33–4
Tasmania 82–3
Tawa 38
technology-/machine-led apocalypse
advanced alien lifeforms
117–18, 119–24
destruction by asteroid 124–8
human loss of control 111–13
life-hating computer
intelligence 112, 115–17
life-hating killer robots 112–15
The Matrix film trilogy 115–17
The Terminator film series
112–13
Temple of Jerusalem 46, 50
'The Terminal Beach' (J. G. Ballard)
134
The Terminator film series 112–13
Thacker, Eugene 70
thinking in the wrong direction
12–14
This Is The End (S. Rogen and
E. Goldberg) 15
The Three-Body Problem (Liu Cixin)
121–2
Thus Spoke Zarathustra
(F. Nietzsche) 151
The Time Machine (H. G. Wells)
130–4, 142, 183
timor mortis 4
Tipler, Frank 149–50
Titus 45–6, 49, 50

Tlapanec people 32
Tolkien, J. R. R. 145
Torah 29
Trump, Donald 86

U
Übermensch, Nietzsche's 153
UN Intergovernmental Panel on
        Climate Change (IPCC)
        162–3, 167
universal heat death 138–42, 153–4,
        183
Utnapishtim 32

V
vampires 72–3
Vermes, Géza 44–5
Vespasian 28–49, 45
video games 9, 65, 88–9, 115,
        174–9
Vishnu 32
von Trier, Lars 126
voodoo 59

W
Wachowski sisters 115–16
Wailing Wall 46
The Walking Dead graphic novel
        and TV series 57–8
Wampanoag people 82
War and Peace (L. Tolstoy) 52
The War of the Worlds (H. G. Wells)
        89, 119–20, 183–4
Ward, Peter 127–8
Wells, H. G. 6, 89, 119–20, 130–4,
        142, 146, 183
Western imperialism 118
When Worlds Collide film and
        novels by (P. Wylie and
        E. Balmer) 125

White Plague (F. Herbert) 88
White Zombie film 59
wildfires 157–8
Williams, William Mattieu 135
Women in Love (D. H. Lawrence)
        96
World of Warcraft series video
        games 175
World War Z: An Oral History
        (M. Brooks) 72
World War Z film 56
Wulfstan, Bishop of London 52

Y
Yucatán Peninsula asteroid hit
        127–8

Z
Zeus 27–9
Zika virus 85
zombie apocalypse 55–7
        alternative names in fiction
                57–8
        bodily and mental decay 73–7
        caused by humans 70–1
        characteristics in popular
                culture 61–2
        comedy 66–7
        consumerism/capitalism 64–5,
                67–70
        decay of society 69–72
        loneliness and grief 72–3
        personification of disease/
                plague 62–3
        slavery and racial
                discrimination 59–61
        survival guides 56
        vampire comparison 63–4
Zombies (R. Luckhurst) 65
Zone One (C. Whitehead) 58